EMPOWERING
THE
heart

Dr. Akil E. Ross
National Principal of the Year

Be Empowered!

D0596900

Reviving & Renewing Today's Education

EMPOWERING THE HEART

Reviving & Renewing Today's Education

by Dr. Akil E. Ross

© 2019 by YouthLight, Inc.
Chapin, SC 29036

All rights reserved. No part of this book may be reproduced or transmitted in any form or by any means, electronic, mechanical, including photocopying, recording, or by any information storage and retrieval system, except in the case of reviews, without the express written permission of the publisher, except where permitted by law.

Cover Design and Project Layout by Amy Rule
Project Editing by Susan Bowman

Library of Congress Control Number
2019937866

ISBN: 978-1-59850-240-4

10 9 8 7 6 5 4 3 2 1
Printed in the United States

PO Box 115 • Chapin, SC 29036
(800) 209-9774 • (803) 345-1070 • Fax (803) 345-0888
yl@youthlightbooks.com • www.youthlight.com

-⩗⩗-TABLE OF CONTENTS-⩗⩗-

⎯⏦⎯ ACKNOWLEDGEMENTS ⏦⎯

Any success a person obtains in life is a result of standing on the shoulders of those who have come before. I am thankful to my faith and church community for the vision, purpose and courage to do all things through Christ. I am grateful to all my teachers who empowered me to reach beyond what I thought possible. Special thanks to Mrs. Shivers who set high expectations for her students and required that our performance met her expectations. I also thank those great administrators and superintendents who gave me a chance to lead. I would like to also thank the Chapin Eagle Family whose teachers, staff, students and parents created an incredible environment for teaching and learning. I am deeply indebted to the Chapin, SC community and community organizations for selflessly supporting our educational process initiatives and for providing the resources needed for our children to thrive. Without the dedication and hard work of my administrative TEAM, I would not have achieved the success I have enjoyed professionally. Special thanks goes to the National Association of Secondary School Principals (NASSP) for their support and continued advocacy for school leaders. I have to thank my editor Kathy Kearse and publishers Bob and Susan Bowman for believing in me and empowering a first time author to tell his story.

Any success a person obtains in life is a result of standing on the shoulders of those who have come before.

I am also grateful for the prayers of my Grandmother Joyce Ross and the counsel of Grandma Anne Wilson. My personal role-model, my Grandfather Ed Wilson showed me the power of hard work. My brother, Azim Ross and I frequently recount his advice to us growing up. "Keep your head in those books," he would say to us. I frequently thought of his words as encouragement to do well in school. Later we realized that, as the grandchild of an enslaved man, this encouragement was a call for freedom.

I thank those who gave me a chance to lead.

To my mother, Patricia Wilson-Ross, I thank you so much for your sacrifice to make sure we had all that we needed. Your focus on education and your high expectations set my brother and me on a trajectory of success.

To my wife and my partner, Jocelyn, thank you for your love, trust and support. You have encouraged me to be better and have made a path for me to do better. Last, I want to thank my children, Alyssa and Akil Jr. "AJ" for understanding why their father is away from home so often and loving him anyway.

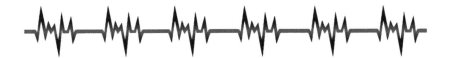

DEDICATION

I dedicate this book to the professional educators who are falling out of love with a profession that is their passion. These educators love the children they serve but are frustrated with a system that is draining their power to educate. These educators are searching for a reason to fall back in love with the profession centered in their hearts. I dedicate this book to the educators who need to be empowered.

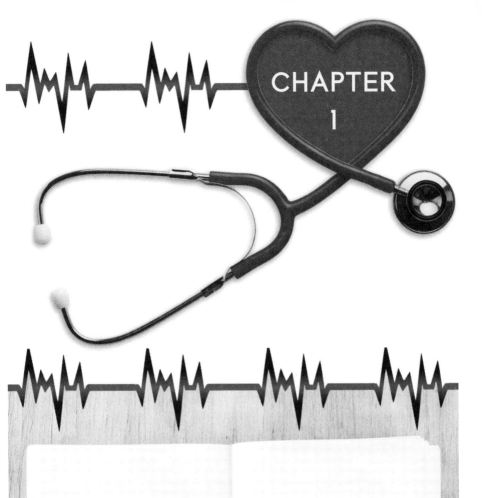

CHAPTER 1

REVIVING THE POWER INSIDE THE HEART

> As we travel along life's journey,
>
> Challenges will come by day and night,
>
> Yet Joy seems tied to conditions,
>
> Absent in the Storm, present in the Light.

"CLEAR!" The familiar voice of the athletic trainer that this veteran principal had known for 14 years was gone. There are war stories in every profession and education is no exception. Yet, I was floored as a fellow principal shared his terrifying experience when his athletic trainer yelled, "Clear! Don't touch his body!" I realized there was no story I had that would match his. The principal explained that he stood at the edge of shock as the automated external defibrillator (AED) charged and delivered a shock to the exposed chest of a spectator who had come to see a high school football game. Moments earlier, the principal was watching the exciting closing moments of the 4th quarter of his school's football playoff game. It was a cool South Carolinian November evening in this small town. The brilliant lights of the stadium illuminated the pitch-black darkness of the surrounding night. The stadium stood out beaconing all to the event. Against the emptiness of the towns' streets, stores, and neighborhoods, the tradition of everyone attending Friday Night Lights was certainly on display this night. The constant ramble of the crowd is segmented by chords from the band, whistles from the officials, the booth announcer and that spontaneous roar of the crowd when there is a big play. Between these sounds, the ramble of the large crowd persisted. That is why the principal did not notice when a staff member ran up to him and asked for the AED. When he realized what was being asked of him, his administrative reflexes sprang into action. He began assessing the situation and calling for help on the radio. When he arrived to the scene, the athletic trainer was in the process of activating the defibrillator.

Real Life Attends Every School

The longer you work in a school, the more you realize there is a disconnect between the way the general public believes educators should perform their duties and what educators really contend with in the performance of their duties. Real life attends every school. Reality is on the class roll of every teacher. The classroom teachers come to work with the goal of ensuring their increasing student case load has not only mastered the numerous standards assigned, but that those students are able to showcase their mastery on the local, state and federal accountability exams. This is a tough goal for the professional educators because not all students learn in the same way or at the same pace. Compounding this challenge is the ever-present effects of reality. Reality is unpredictable, emotional and consuming. The daily reality of poverty, discrimination, geopolitics, bullying, classroom disruptions, cyber offenses, substance abuse, emotional and physical abuse, suicides and school shootings are ever present. These realities take their toll. There are times the constant realities can leave today's educators feeling powerless.

Powerless Yet Accountable

After the first charge was delivered to the patient, the AED advised cardiopulmonary resuscitation (CPR). As the athletic trainer started the chest compressions, the principal stood in disbelief that the shock of electricity delivered to this man's body had not revived him.

Emotions began to overcome him as he realized a man may lose his life while at a school-sponsored event. Principals are responsible for everything that occurs on the campus. Effective principals give credit for the success of the school and take responsibility for the failures on the campus. This was a very effective principal. His school has been recognized on a state and national level for school leadership and academic achievement. Now, he stood there powerless to save this man's life. He radioed the appropriate personnel, set into motion the medical safety plan, cleared the area for emergency personnel and informed district officials. Faced with a reality of this magnitude, the principal, like most educators today, are forced to stand powerless to solve the problem yet still accountable for the problem. To be powerless is a problem for the heart.

This book is written for those educators whose hearts are troubled because of the feelings of powerlessness to save the futures of the children for whom they are accountable and responsible. There are teachers, counselors, assistants, school staff and administrators who arrive to campus each day to the growing realization that the pulse of their passion for educating is fading away. As an educator, I empathize with those in need of a revival of their professional passion because they have succumb to the stifling demands of accountability and the ever-increasing workload that drains energy. I empathize with those feeling powerless to do anything to bring relief.

The frustrations that educators face are growing inside the school and outside of school. The September 2018 *Time Magazine* cover story featured teacher Hope Brown from Woodford County High School in Versailles, Kentucky. The story title "I have a master's degree, 16 years of experience, work two extra jobs and donate plasma to pay the bills. I'm a teacher in America" (Reilly, 2018) gives insight into the feeling of powerlessness that many teachers experience. The author Katie Reilly cites that the average teacher salary is 24% lower than careers of other college graduates, yet the requirements and responsibilities are considerable and continue to increase. More teachers are showing up to work drained from the stress of working two jobs, caring for children and parents, managing sky rocketing cost of living, dealing with health issues and living one pay check to another. As a result, we are losing teachers and school personnel from schools at record rates. This book provides a practical framework that refocuses school systems to empower educators by empowering students.

Losing Power

How do you manage your power? A person manages their power similar to the way he or she manages the fuel in their automobile. There is a universal dashboard gauge in motor vehicles that indicates the amount of fuel remaining in the gas tank. The driver is informed by a needle on this dashboard gauge of the fuel level as it passes five distinct points; full, ¾ tank, ½ tank, ¼ tank and E. The "E" stands for empty.

There are some drivers who immediately look for a fueling station when the needle on the dashboard fuel gauge hits the ½ tank mark. These drivers understand that allowing the fuel tank to run lower than ½ tank without refueling will place them in jeopardy of running out of power. These people seek to prepare themselves for the unexpected events of life. They understand that traffic delays and detours can drain more power than what had previously been planned. As a result, as soon as the needle on the fuel indicator hits ½ tank, they seek refueling.

On the other end of the spectrum, there are those drivers who wait until the needle hits the "E" before they entertain the thought of refueling. These drivers should not be mistaken for poor planners or irresponsible drivers. They are more concerned with the internal traffic, delays and detours in their minds than the external conditions of the road. They have been lulled into a false sense of security because of an additional dashboard feature called range. In most motor vehicles, the driver can hit a button and get the range of the vehicle. The range will tell the driver approximately how long the vehicle can travel before the vehicle is totally out of fuel. The "E" driver depends on this vital feature. If this feature indicates the vehicle has a range of 10 miles and the highway sign says the next fueling station is 5 miles away, then the driver is confident in this vehicle's ability to have enough power to be refueled.

What happens when those numbers are reversed? The dashboard says the range is 5 miles, but the highway sign says the next fueling station is 10 miles away! I have been in that position. This is an extremely stressful position to find yourself. Immediately, I began to reduce power. I cut off the radio, unplugged the cellphone from the charger, turned off the air conditioning, rolled the windows down in hopes that the wind could assist in pushing the car (now I realize how illogical that was). I even asked the kids in the back seat to be quiet because somehow I felt their talking was draining fuel. I could feel my heart pounding. Beads of sweat were forming on my head faster than I could wipe them. I prayed for relief, "Lord, just let me make it to this gas station. I promise I will never do this again. I don't care how much I have to pay for this gas, just don't let me run out of fuel!" The dashboard now reads, "Range Low" and I can see the marquee of the gas station over the horizon. "If I can just make it to...", then it dawned on me. This is not the only time I have felt this way.

Finding Power

As a teacher, coach, assistant principal, principal and district office administrator, I have come to those points of time during the school year where I have said, "If I can just make it to...", the blank is filled in with so many distant events like Labor Day, Thanksgiving, Christmas and winter break, MLK holiday, spring break, and the summer break. Some of my colleagues would start count down clocks as soon as we came back from a holiday. Ever present throughout the school year is the "If I can just make it to Friday" statement. Most "If" statements are accompanied by a "then" statement. The science teacher calls it a hypothesis and the English teacher calls it a conditional statement. Either way, the "If/Then" statement is true when both parts of the statement are met. Truth is, educators do make it to Friday (even though some have often taken that day off), yet they make the same statement again in the next week. As a result, the hypothesis is false! The "If I can make it to Friday," statement assumes the "Then" statement is, "I will be refueled." In reality there is a growing majority of educators who are running low on fuel and are at-risk of completely running out of power.

Power is required to do work. When you are powerless, the work you intend to do goes undone. This book provides hope for those educators exhausted from the continual condition of powerlessness they experience in the classrooms and hallways of our schools. This book provides an easy-to-use framework that will lead educators off the road of powerlessness and guide them along the refreshing and reviving route to empowerment. A study reported by the University Council for Educational Administration (Fuller, 2018), stated that the conditions of the schools were the leading cause of teachers leaving the profession. In a time of severe teacher shortages and growing dissatisfaction with the conditions of education, our schools need to be refueled, revived and renewed.

The key to this renewal lies in the same strategy that helped me get to the gas station when I was on "E." When I was running out of fuel, praying to make it to the gas station, I started to clear out certain functions that were not essential to the ride or the destination. I cut off the radio, air conditioning, and battery charger. Anything that was draining power and not essential to the ride or the destination was cleared. The same is true for schools. Educators need all tasks not essential to the true vision of education CLEARED away so that their efforts and energy can be used to maximize the potential of the children. This book begins by refocusing on the destination. It is easier to make it to the end of the tunnel when you see the light. When I saw the fueling station, I felt that I could make it. The number one problem we face in schools is the vision problem. Chapters 2 & 3 will outline a clear vision for effective education. Chapters 4 & 5 remind educators of the essentials we truly need for the "ride" in our schools. These chapters give the reader simple and easy-to-implement strategies that will improve teaching and learning from day one. The "gas gauge" of the book lies in Chapters 6 & 7. These chapters help us understand how well we are educating our children by the degree in which they are empowered. Finally, Chapters 8 & 9 come from my last graduation speech as a high school principal. It is a message about the most important lesson each student should have learned before leaving school. This message provides all children with an empowerment tool that will help them when the storms of life have them on "E." This book is designed to give school leaders the skills for empowering students and faculty in all schools.

Searching for the Heart

The AED began to reassess the patient's status and advised a second shock! The principal remembered from his Red Cross training that there are only 3 electrical shocks in each unit and now this man was on his second. He had collapsed at the visitor's concession stand and amid this very emotional scene the principal could still hear that constant ramble of the crowd. The crowd, players and coaches were not even aware that someone's life was on the line. With all the activity of the football game continuing, the principal was informed that the man had no pulse. The man was clinically dead. The term clinically dead is a medical term to describe when a person's heart stops beating. The voice of the AED instructed everyone to stand clear of the patient's body. The athletic trainer yelled "CLEAR!" The stress of the fight to revive the man had overcome her normal voice. The AED charges and the second shock is delivered through the pads on the chest of the patient. The jolt of the man's body is the only indication that the electricity had been delivered. "Praise GOD!" yelled the Principal. There were signs of sustained movement. The man began moving under his own power and actually attempted to sit up! As the principal retold the story, he concluded by saying, "That man was gone; the shock to the heart brought him back to life."

The heart is the source of life for the body. It's our power source both biologically and spiritually. The love of teaching and learning is dying out for many educators and it's time for an educational defibrillation to revive the passion and motivation for the classroom teacher, school administrator, parent, community and student. Just like the AED shocks the heart back into normal rhythms, this book provides an educational framework to shock our school system back to its true mission.

I had the opportunity to interview Kenyon Wells, the former CEO of a medical supplies company which sells the AEDs used to revive the man at the game. He shared that the AED searches for the rhythm of the heart and assesses how far from a normal heart beat rhythm a person has in order to deliver the correct amount of power. There is no standard shock. Each patient has a distinct heart rhythm. Life and death hinges on the AEDs ability to find the heart's rhythm. As educators, we save lives in almost the same way. When we search the heart of a child, we can discover the individual needs that have to be met as well as the passions that should be developed. Only then are we empowered to maximize the potential of that child. The goal of this book is to empower educators, so they can empower students.

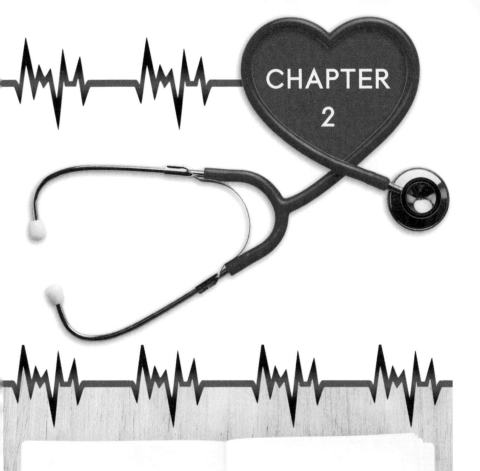

CHAPTER 2

RETHINKING THE PURPOSE OF SCHOOL

> For the Storm knows its mission,
>
> The Wind, Rain and Thunder have joined its ranks,
>
> The Storm comes to steal your Joy,
>
> In its midst, Are YOU empowered to give thanks?

"I don't know who I am." I was actually relieved by the honesty in this high school senior's reply. In May of each year, I conducted senior interviews. Due to the growing number of students in the senior class, I was not able to speak to all seniors. However, the cross section of candidates for graduation I interviewed ranged from the lowest performing student in the class to the class valedictorian. Each senior was invited to the principal's office for an exit interview. For some, this was their very first time in the Principal's Office and they had to be reassured they were not in trouble. Others were quite comfortable and made themselves at home on the couch that flanked the courtyard window in my office. Opposite the couch were two chairs with a coffee table between them. The intent of this office layout was to create a living room feeling for student and parent meetings. It is amazing the influence the setting can have on the emotions of people. Sitting at a conference table created formal conversations and I rarely felt I made a personal connection with the person on the other side. On the contrary, the living room office layout created an informal setting and invoked feelings of a home visit. Students and parents would assume a more relaxed position and stretch out. Some would even put their feet up. The resulting conservations almost always concluded on amicable terms.

The school secretary notified me that the next appointment had arrived. In walked the valedictorian (the student with the highest-grade point average at the time of the interview). These interviews were intended to collect data that was not available through the traditional surveys. Those surveys typically measure how students feel about the instructional quality of the school. The surveys ask how safe a student feels at the school, their feelings toward the teachers and administrators, and the accessibility of school resources like technology, instructional materials and extracurricular activities. In short, the data from these surveys gave me information about the health of the school. However, these one-on-one interviews were intended to gain insight about the social-emotional health of the child. I asked each student two questions. **(1) "Who are you?"** and **(2) "What does fail-ure mean to you?"** It was this young man's response to the first question that took the conversation in another direc-tion. When I asked the valedictorian "Who are you?" I could see him struggle to find a response. His shoulders slumped, his head dropped and in a sunken voice, he answered, "I don't know who I am." It's not what he said that bothered me because many young adults have no answer for this ques-tion. What troubled me was how he answered. He did not look at me. There was no personal connection. All the plan-ning I did to set up my office so that the living room layout could create a meaningful connection did not produce the usual comfort effect. He was not happy. He was the valedictorian! I thought all valedictorians were happy.

This student completed 12 years of school and never made a grade less than an "A" and all of his teachers had nothing but praise and compliments for his work and work ethic. He was an accomplished musician and a leader in the school band. He was enrolled in Advanced Placement (AP) classes and passed each AP test. He was recognized nationally as a National Merit Finalist and two questions shy of a perfect score on the Scholastic Assessment Test (SAT). This was a very accomplished student, and now he was stumped on a question that should have been easily answered. This student was wise enough to know that the answer I sought was not his name, grades, test scores, extracurriculars or demographics because that information is available to any principal in the school database. He knew that the question asked of him was something he spent little study on. However, it is a question he should have mastered before all other subjects.

How is it that the highest performing student comes to the last days of school and is unable to answer a question that a child in elementary school should be able to answer with enthusiasm? I was proud of his honesty yet bothered by the way he gave the answer. Most students answer, the "Who are you?" question by describing what they want to be when they grow up. Others answer the question by outlining their plans after graduation. They offer as answers their college major, technical school training or military service. These answers refer to the future, but the question is about the present. With tears in his eyes, the valedictorian faced a cold reality. He could not identify his purpose in life because there was no purpose in his present. I always knew something was missing from the education system. It was at this moment, I realized what the process of schooling omitted. As a teacher, I wanted to build the mind of the student. As a coach, I wanted to strengthen the body of the athlete. Omitted from the formal schooling process was the building up and strengthening of the spirit of the child.

Why Do We Have Schools?

During a faculty and staff meeting, I asked the group of 170 teachers, support staff, custodians, cafeteria staff, school counselors and administrators, "Why do you come to work?" I have always believed that a person's internal motivation will determine their external actions. Author, Simon Sinek advised leaders to know the purpose of their organization in his book, *Start With Why?*, so I decided to inquire about the collective purpose of this high school. With the assistance of the media center staff, we were able to collect a response from each person. Then we displayed the ideas of the group in a word cloud (see the illustration).

In a word cloud, the responses that are repeated by the group most often appear larger than the words repeated with less frequency. This was a unique tool for understanding the collective feelings and ideas of the faculty. I had no idea what the result would be when I asked the question. I gave up total control of creating the vision of the school so that the faculty and staff could establish a collective vision. This can be uncomfortable for some administrators. I was blessed to have a faculty and staff that were smarter than I was. Their answers proved they were spot-on correct. The collective purpose was not about pay, retirement, testing, graduation rates, attendance rates or any of the other variables used to measure schools. These teachers stated clearly; they come to work for the students! The next largest word in the word cloud was "prepare" followed by "life" with "productive" being the 4th most frequently stated word. From this, we made the following vision statement:

"WE PREPARE ALL STUDENTS
FOR PRODUCTIVE LIVES"

This became our collective purpose and the vision of my administration for the duration of my career. The reality is that schools have always existed to prepare our country for future needs. In the late 1700s, Noah Webster led the charge to prepare a literate citizenry in order to preserve the republic. In the mid 1800s, Horace Mann and his Common Schools prepared children to obtain the American Dream. In the early 1900s, the social changes of the nation caused schools to prepare students to be Americanized and Industrialized. Until his death, in 1952, John Dewey argued that schools should prepare to humanize students by allowing the child to learn through experience (Goldin, 1999). After the launch of Sputnik in 1957, schools were transformed to prepare students to compete in math and science on a global stage. Today's schools are preparing students to be accountable to the state's accountability policy. An October 24, 2015 report from the *Washington Post* stated that the average student in big-city schools was administered 112 mandatory tests between prekindergarten and 12th grade (Layton, 2015). Without doing justice to the history of education reform in the United States, there have been considerable shifts in the philosophy of how best to prepare our students. As a result of these shifts, changes and swings in educational philosophy, school systems are filled with a diverse array of attitudes about the purpose and mission of education. Even on my campus, I had some of the most essentialistic teachers in the world. If passing was 60% and the grade averaged out to 59.99%, these teachers would argue emphatically that the child should repeat the class. On the other end of the spectrum, I had some of the most progressive teachers. Their classes were usually outside, doing projects and coloring things. I would have to almost beg these teachers to give a test with increased rigor. The point is, the faculty lived along a philosophical continuum. Consequently, I was excited about having a common vision. The challenge would be creating a common mission. I needed to ask myself the same question that stumped the valedictorian, "Who am I?"

Are We Educators?

There are two different meanings for the word "educate." The duality of the term comes from the two Latin roots. The first Latin root is "Educare" which means to train. This is the definition of education that is most familiar. School personnel use standards, curricula, courses of study, credits, transcripts, seat time and grades as the framework for the training of students. When students pass a class, they are assumed to have retained the information outlined in the standards. This prerequisite knowledge is intended to serve as a foundation for the next level of standards and curriculum. However, when the student passes the class and the prerequisite material is not retained, then the instructional foundation is compromised. If part of the purpose of education is to train a child, then we must examine how we train our students. One summer, I reviewed all of our state's educational standards and indicators for the 9th grade subjects of English, Mathematics, Science and Social Studies. I found that these subjects averaged 45 standards per course. That means a freshman has 180 days (the length of the school year) to learn 180 standards and this does not include standards and objectives in World Languages, Art, Physical Education, Career & Technical education as well as other electives. This reality caused me to question our training methods because it is unrealistic to ask students to keep this pace. Not only does mastering a standard per day seem unrealistic, but the task is also further complicated by the number of days taken away from instruction for testing, school wide events and mandatory training.

A Better Way

I was radioed to come to my office. When I arrived, I found a teacher with tears in her eyes. This frustrated teacher had come to find me during her planning period. Too upset to sit down on my couch, she said, "I can't do what you are asking me to do. I am a good teacher. I know I am!" Her face was red. Her voice quivering holding back the tears. This was one of my best teachers. "Mrs. Banner, what's wrong? How can I help?" I asked. If one of my most effective teachers is on the verge of quitting, then the entire faculty could be at the brink of quitting because they are overwhelmed. "I simply can not teach all of the concepts, objectives and standards you expect of me!" She felt herself losing control and took a seat on the couch. She began to take deep breaths. Her voice returned to its normal register. While she apologized for becoming emotional, I could tell she felt justified in her actions. She reached the point where she could no longer cope with the conditions in which she had been placed. What was worse, her principal had no clue of the severity of her experience. Instead of listening to the teacher so I could draw a solution from her perspective, I decided to spring into action and solve the problem myself. This would prove to be a huge mistake.

I heard about the "stations" instructional strategy used in elementary schools. I figured I would adapt it for a high school U.S. History Class so that I could teach more material with limited time. Instead of seeking proper training on this strategy, I felt time was of the essence and as the principal, I had to save this teacher. I told her that I would teach one of her classes and show her how she could effectively teach three indicators in one 90-minute class. She laughed. While I was relieved in the change of her mood, I was a little offended that she would laugh at the thought of the principal teaching her class. "Are you sure you want to do this?" asked Mrs. Banner still chuckling. My competitive spirit got the best of me, and I doubled down. "Not only will I teach the class, but also I want you and the assistant principal in charge of instruction to complete a classroom observation form so that others can learn this strategy from my example." I went all-in! There was no turning back. "I can't wait to see this," Mrs. Banner said with a smile on her face. She was starting a new unit in a week and asked that I kick off the new unit. That very afternoon, she sent me the pacing guide and standards for the class I would teach.

I had over a week to prepare for one class. I spent two days on the presentation, two days on the art activity (for cross-curricular pedagogy), and another day gathering materials for the group activity. I literally spent 5 days to prepare for one class. The pacing guide provided by the Central Office called for students to learn about Urbanization in the United States, The Great Migration, and the Jazz Age, all in 90 minutes! I could teach an entire course on the Jazz Age alone. On the day of the class, I used my principal powers to ensure there were no disruptions from fire drills, announcements, or office calls. Teachers, hearing about my attempt to be an "effective" teacher (after being out of the classroom for over a decade), lined up in the hall to witness this attempt first hand. I would not let them see me sweat but I was a nervous wreck. "What did I get myself into?" I thought to myself.

I greeted the students at the door as they arrived. When the bell rang, there were stragglers. My own policy required that they receive a tardy pass, but I had too much material to cover – there was no time. I briefly explained what I was trying to do today, but I couldn't get into the details because there was no time for explanation. I started to take the roll and asked students to begin the reflection question that was on the board. A student asked about the details of a school sporting event and I redirected him to the assignment because there was no time. A young lady asked permission to go to the attendance office; I told her to hurry up because there was no time. Looking at my watch, it was already 10 minutes into the class and I felt the pressure of not being able to get to all my activities. I began to implement the lesson as planned. I explained the stations and the task for each station. Students were very uncomfortable with changing the format of the class. They did not say it aloud but body language revealed their discomfort with the change. This lesson was dying a slow death. I glanced over at the teacher and assistant principal and they looked extremely unimpressed. Each activity required so much explanation and context but there was no time. Students' hands began to spring up across the class. "I don't understand. What are we supposed to be doing? Can you help me? Do you have another copy of this sheet? Can I go to the restroom?" There was no time for any of these things. I found myself racing from one random question about the lesson to another. Each answer was surface level. Students asked questions to get the correct answer and not to learn. I failed to hook students into the concept and challenge them to independently evaluate their learning because there was no time. I noticed the class was about to end when the students started packing up and I did my best to bring closure to the three objectives for the day. At the end of the class, when the students left, Mrs. Banner placed her hand on my shoulder in a consoling manner and said, "You tried your best." I had the perfect conditions for teaching this lesson. I had 5 days of planning, the authority to suspend any student who disrupted the class, I even controlled the school calendar to ensure there would be no interruptions to my class, yet I could not manage to present all that information in the time allotted. There was no time.

It took a first-hand experience like this for me to realize that students are not able to keep up with the pace and are certainly not retaining all of this information. *The Forgetting Curve* by Hermann Ebbinghaus illustrates that after one month of hearing new information we remember about 10% of the material (Weiss, 2017). Therefore, we were not training students to learn and retain information. We were training them to hold information long enough until it was needed for a test. We were not preparing students with skills to be productive in life. We were preparing them only to be successful in school. Maybe my valedictorian did not know who he was because we, the educators, forgot our role in preparing him for his whole life.

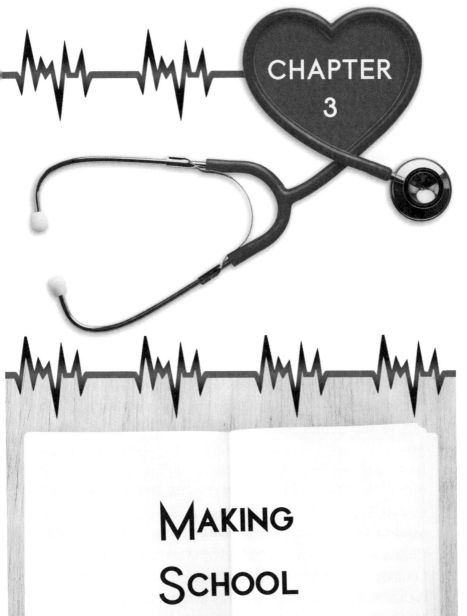

MAKING
SCHOOL
MEANINGFUL

From where does this power come,

The answer is one of three parts,

We are Mind, Body and Spirit

The latter powers our Hearts.

"He needs a boost." said Cheryl, the school secretary. Before the senior meeting with the valedictorian, the school secretary stepped into my office and closed the door behind her. Whispering so that the student outside could not hear our conservation, Cheryl explained that the valedictorian needed some help. Like many principals, I benefited tremendously from the hard work and dedication of the support staff. From the front office receptionist and bookkeeper to the athletics secretary and school nurse, the school support staff is vital to the success of the school. Their ability to catch what falls between the cracks makes them essential to the mission of any school. As such, Cheryl was extremely talented at identifying students and families who deserved to be praised and recognized, as well as seeking out the students in need of motivation and inspiration. Without her assistance, I never would have known about the internal conflict inside of the school's top performing student.

Cheryl handed me the student's transcript and report card. I looked at the transcript, the academic history of a student's performance in courses issuing Carnegie Units. For this student, it was very impressive. He received all "A's" in the rigorous honors and Advanced Placement courses. I immediately noticed his grade point average (GPA) which was over 5.0 and made a joke about how he could cut his GPA in half and it would still be higher than a lot of other students. Cheryl did not laugh. "Dr. Ross, look at his report card," she said as she turned my attention to the second sheet of paper. She highlighted his GPA for the year. I could not believe what I was seeing. The third quarter grades had fallen below the "A" level and one course was a "C!" I was in disbelief. I wondered how a student with this academic history could come to such a pass in the second semester of his final year in high school. I told Cheryl this is the worst case of senioritis (a condition when high school seniors lose motivation to do work because their previous grades guarantee graduation) I had ever seen and I was grateful he was on the senior interview list. "I'll let you two talk," Cheryl said as she opened the door and ushered the student into my office.

As I described earlier, the valedictorian teared up when confronted with my first senior interview question "Who are you?" and acknowledged that he did not know how to answer this question. His reaction led me to question my assumption about him having senioritis. Most 12th graders are prone to lose motivation in the spring before graduation. They begin to complain about the work load and assignments. These students will sometimes have a noticeable drop in performance due to a decrease in school attendance, studying and effort on assignments. Nevertheless, students with senioritis do not tear up when questioned about their performance. There was more going on with this student. I wondered...could this young man be depressed?

Students Are Losing Power

I am not trained to diagnose the mental state of a student. However, educators are trained to look for signs of stress and discomfort in our students. Some schools are fortunate enough to have access to social workers, school counselors, school psychologists, and other mental health professionals who assist school personnel in diagnosing, treating and/or referring students with mental health concerns. While I was fortunate to have access to these personnel, I cannot imagine how schools operate without these resources. The need for healthy social-emotional development in today's schools may be the greatest challenge facing the future outcomes of students in the country. Millions of children today are not equipped to face adversity in life. As a result, these children have come to rely on negative coping strategies such as:

the condition of the emotions and all blood flows from the heart. As a result, the heart must be the center of the spirit. In order to educate the whole child, each school must be intentional about reaching the inside of each child by leading from the heart.

In Search for the Heart

I have a unique method for teaching students how to improve their abilities to cope with adversity. My methodology does not come from an intensive study of psychotherapy. On the contrary, I have been influenced by a movie that was based upon a children's book. In 1900, Lyman Frank Baum published *The Wonderful Wizard of Oz*. In 1939, MGM produced the blockbuster movie *The Wizard of Oz*. The movie chronicles the journey of Dorothy Gale, played by Judy Garland, on her quest to return to her home in Kansas, after being uprooted by a tornado, to the Land of Oz. She is advised to meet the Wizard who will be able to help her return home. The path to the Wizard is along the yellow brick road. Sparing a summary of the entire story, there is one scene that resonated with me as an instructional leader. Dorothy meets three characters on the yellow brick road, but only one of the characters was human. After meeting the Scarecrow and before she met the Cowardly Lion, Dorothy comes across something in the forest and says, "Why it's a man. A man made out of tin." How can a man be made of tin? The Tin Man played by Jack Haley explains that he is made out of tin, and he has no heart. "It's empty," said the Tin Man referring to his body or chest cavity. "The Tinsmith forgot to give me a heart." For the rest of the movie, there is no other mention of how the Tinsmith was able to turn a human into a tin machine.

Teaching the Tin Man

The story of the Tin Man's transformation is outlined in the book entitled, *The Marvelous Land of Oz*. Published in 1904, this was the second book of L. Frank Baum's fourteen book Oz series. In the text, we learn the Tin Man was born Nick Chopper, a normal man. He grew up in the forest and was a lumberjack by trade. One day while chopping trees, his axe becomes enchanted and cuts off his arm. Nick Chopper goes to the Tinsmith and asks for his arm to be repaired. The Tinsmith explains his craft to Nick Chopper. The Tinsmith does not have the ability to fix a human arm, but he does have the skills to make him a shiny new arm out of tin. Nick Chopper agrees to this procedure, which leaves Nick with one human arm and one shiny tin mechanized arm.

The next day Nick Chopper hikes back out into the forest to chop down more trees. He discovers that his new mechanized arm performs much better than the human arm. The mechanized tin arm is stronger than the human arm; moreover, it does not get tired or ache after a long day. The Tin Man has an idea. If he has two tin arms, then he will be able to cut down more trees than any other lumberjack in the forest. So Nick Chopper does the unthinkable. With his enchanted axe, he sacrifices his other arm. Nick Chopper goes back to the Tinsmith and receives a new tin arm. With two tin arms, Nick Chopper's thoughts are confirmed. He is now able to cut down more trees than any woodman in the forest. He is soon dissatisfied. His enchanted axe goes back to work and takes one leg. He goes to the Tinsmith and asks for a tin leg. He does not stop there. He sacrifices his other leg with the enchanted axe and asks Tinsmith for another tin mechanized leg. With tin limbs and a human body, Nick Chopper is still not satisfied. His legs and his arms are mechanized and can work with amazing efficiency. However, the body still needs food, water and rest. Nick Chopper, looking at the possibility of increased efficiency and output, decides to sacrifice his entire body for a shiny new tin body.

However, without a heart, Nick Chopper is no longer able to experience feelings. He has lost his emotional connection with anyone including his loved ones. Nick Chopper sees his value in his work as a woodman and as a result, he is satisfied with his sacrifice because an increase in lumber productivity means an increase in his value. Without a heart, Nick Chopper makes his next decision with ease. He decides to give the Tinsmith his head. No human would think to sacrifice their head, but without a heart, this seems to be a logical decision for him. Now with a full shiny tin mechanized body, there is no more Nick Chopper. He is now the Tin Woodman. He forgets who he was. The Tin Woodman is only concerned with the work and increased productivity. He works constantly and even when the rains come, he keeps working. He chops and chops until the rain rusts him and his mechanized tin parts can no longer move. He stays there for ages until found by Dorothy.

The Power In The Heart

L. Frank Baum wrote the Oz series during a radical change in the American economic and social condition. The age of agriculture was confronted with industrialization and mass production. There were many advances and social benefits from "these changes." The economy grew and the goods available in the marketplace kept up with the pace of growth. Upon closer inspection, the focus on the increased outcomes led to the neglect of the people who worked in the factories. Before the labor movement, the work day could be as long as fourteen hours and the work week six days. Even children were used to increase productivity in the factories.

In fact, children are still used to increase productivity. They are used in the education system to drive the ever-increasing demand for high test scores and graduation rates. While these products or school outcomes are intended to benefit the children, some researchers are now questioning the role the heavy focus on outcomes plays on the emotional health of students. In his book, *At What Cost?*, Dr. David Gleason, a clinical psychologist, chronicles the attitudes and behaviors of students around the world in competitive high schools. He states that "anxiety, depression and their dangerous manifestations – substance abuse, eating disorders, self-injury and suicide – are increasing student conditions at many competitive high schools." Dr. Gleason found that "...dedicated adults fully admit to over-scheduling, overworking and at times, overwhelming their students and teenage children" (Gleason, 2017). I argue that the drive for increased productivity has created these conditions at all schools.

While the Tin Man was rusted to a halt and unable to work, he could still think. This reflection time gave him the opportunity to focus on something other than the outcomes and productivity. I imagine this reflection time allowed him to remember Nick Chopper, his human self. There is power in reflection. Having the ability to step away from the machine of work and evaluate the purpose of the work is essential for healthy growth. The rusted Tin Man transformed his way of thinking. Likewise, instead of being the administrator focused on organization, processes and production, he became a behavioral scientist. In behavioral science the leader uses critical thinking and analysis to evaluate more than how much is being produced, but why they are producing it. The behavioral scientist wonders about the effects of his production on the environment, his neighbors and himself. The behavioral scientist does not rely on large data sets, charts, graphs and survey data to make a decision, yet employs case and field studies to build a deeper understanding of the people represented by numbers and percentages. The Tin Man in his new role as a behavioral scientist was empowered to ask himself the question, "Who am I?" Through the power of reflection in the behaviorist lens the Tin Man must have concluded that the moment he lost his humanity was the moment he sacrificed his heart. Therefore, when Dorothy finds him after "ages" of reflection time, he declares, "If I only had a heart…"

My "depressed valedictorian" like most of his peers needed time for personal reflection. He needed to move away from the overwhelming, ever-increasing demands for production in grades, test scores, and activities designed to bolster his resume. He needed time to reflect on the question, "Who am I?" If schools focused their instructional goals around the abilities of students to engage in critical analysis, we would find that more students could answer this question. They would first come to the realization that the answer to the question is in the present tense. So much of the focus of K-12 education is preparing students for graduation. Consequently, it is easy to lose sight of who the students are in the present.

There is power in the present because the present is the only time when you can experience joy. Your gift is in your heart. "For as he thinketh in his heart, so is he..." (Proverbs 23:7, KJV). When we connect our children to their hearts, we bring them joy. When our children are empowered to use their gifts to bring others joy, it empowers us. The word valedictorian comes from the Latin root, "valedicere" which means to bid farewell. It does not mean highest grade point average. Imagine the positive impact on the emotional conditions of our children, if the position of honor at graduation did not go to the highest producer of grades, but to the best story of growth and personal development. That would be a farewell address that would educate us all.

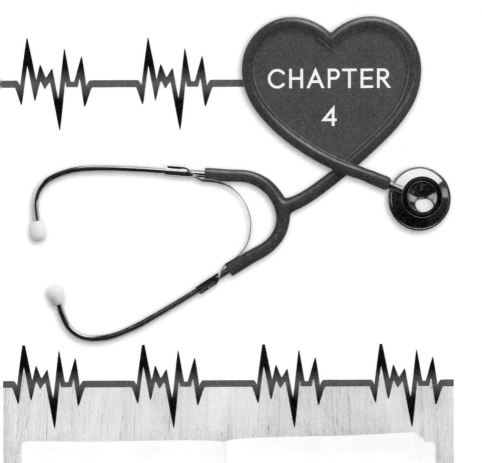

CHAPTER
4

DISCOVERING HOW
F.A.I.L. SPELLS
SUCCESS

> The goal of education, let me overview
>
> By the end of schooling I pray you knew,
>
> The question, to the mirror, Who Are You?
>
> Learning is not something just to get through
>
> The process matters in the things you do,
>
> So when you fail once, smile on take two,
>
> For the purpose of life, inside is the best clue,
>
> Our heart has the power, that we appeal to.

"He failed the third grade. Now he's the best high school principal in the nation." This was the headline of Tim Flach's article in *The State*, a major newspaper in South Carolina. To be honest, I was not happy with the title. The article covered my greatest professional achievement, receiving the National School Principal of the Year award from NASSP (National Association for Secondary School Principals) but this article's title also brought to light one of my greatest failures. Repeating a grade is not like most failures. Most failures or mistakes in life can be easily forgotten because they are private, and the consequences of that failure are short term. Everyone has failures. These are often embarrassing moments in our lives to which we do not want to draw attention. For example, I was walking down a hallway I have traveled hundreds of times. This particular time I had failed to clear the metal plate at the base of the fire door and I took the longest stumble of my entire life. It seemed like I would never be able to regain my balance as I stammered down the hallway. Trying not to add sound effects to this disgusting display, I was only thinking about one thing. I hope no one is watching me. I did not have a problem tripping. I did not mind falling. I feared that one of the 1400 students in that building would record me tripping and falling and then post that video clip on social media for likes and reposts. I worried that by the end of the day my embarrassing moment would go viral on social media.

Before the prevalence of social media, it took a lot of energy, time and effort to spread a story. Whether a good story or a bad story, without social media it was easier for a celebration or an incident to die out and not be told again. For a child that repeats a grade, their embarrassing failure can be told on any day of that year. It was tough to explain why I was older and much taller than my peers. It was tough to explain why it took me two years to master material most children could in one year. It was tough for me to explain why I failed. So at the age of ten, I concluded that I was dumb. I had plenty of evidence to support my conclusion. I did not fail the second grade but that year I was a failure. I attended a school in the suburbs of Maryland, which bordered Washington, DC. As an African American male, I was in the minority in terms of race. I soon came to learn I was also in the minority in terms of my academic ability.

It seemed to me that all the other students learned faster and knew more than I did. I withdrew from the academic process and decided my rewards would come from other pursuits. Despite the amazing efforts of my second-grade teacher, I decided to assume the role of class clown. Making people laugh gave me positive attention from my classmates. I received many reprimands for disrupting class. It was better to receive attention for something bad than to receive no attention at all. Unfortunately, I did not receive academic skills either.

In October of the next year, my mother moved my brother and me to Northeast Washington, D.C. and I enrolled in Jesse LaSalle Elementary School. I entered a third grade classroom packed with students. There was one more desk available in the class and I can still remember how uncomfortable I was getting settled into it. After the teacher introduced me as the new student, she began the lesson. I was lost. I had no clue what they were doing. I had been in this space before and decided to try my hand at the class clown role. Instantly, I realized that position was occupied by two students bigger than me and they were in no mood to allow any competition. I remembered feeling helpless. All my efforts were in vain. Every assignment I turned in was consistently marked "F." I still remember the look on the teacher's face when I would turn in assignments. It was like I was disappointing her on purpose. My best work was not on par with the rest of the class and we both had little expectations that my work would get better. I was soon moved into a remediation class that pulled me out of the regularly scheduled class. In this new class, I received assistance intended to help me stay on course with my class-mates. I relied heavily on the remediation teacher, but she had five others in that classroom who required the same assistance maybe more due to the fact that three of the other students were immigrants. This frustration continued the entire year. Concluding I was dumb, I did nothing to prevent being retained in the third grade for the next year. I felt deeply that I was a failure.

That summer my mother met with the principal and asked that I be placed in the class of the most effective teacher in the 3rd grade. This request was granted. I was placed in Mrs. Shivers' class. Rumor had it that Mrs. Shivers was thrown out of the Marine Corps because she had made the soldiers cry. Consequently, they assigned her to teach third grade in the DC public school system (the rumor made perfect sense to a 10-year-old). Mrs. Shivers was a no-nonsense kind of teacher. She made her expectations extremely clear and did not compromise them. Mrs. Shivers' expec-tations extended past her student's academic ability. She demanded the highest expectation for your speech, your behavior in the classroom, your behavior outside of the classroom, your dress code, and even in the way that you walked. We were instructed to walk on the right of the hall-way and to maneuver in the halls at 90-degree angles like soldiers. Any deviation from her expectations led to a swift consequence. After the consequence, Mrs. Shivers would require us to practice more of what we initially failed to do.

Are Students Too Big to F.A.I.L. (Face Adversity In Life)?

During the financial crisis of 2008, we learned of institutions whose success was so essential to the overall health of the economy that their failure would be fatal to the economic system. These institutions were called "Too Big To Fail." *New York Times* columnist, Andrew Ross Sorkin stated, "We talk about institutions that are too big to fail. I think the story is as much about people who think they are too big to fail." For many students, that low test score or failing grade is a name. It implies they are failures and have jeopardized their futures. The sight of an "F" on a test or report card means that no college scholarships and admission letters will be offered. As a result, instead of learning from these lessons, they seek a "bail out." An "Educational Bail Out" is not to be confused with an Educational Accommodation. Accommodations and modifications in education are used to level the playing field. An "Educational Bail Out" gives a student an unnecessary advantage. The bail out safeguards students from failure by creating conditions in which others provide supports that make it almost impossible to fail.

As a principal, I have had many meetings with parents and students about failing grades or low test scores and the conversation has little to do with the student's ability to perform a skill or understand a concept. These conversations evoke strong emotions from families and usually lead to blaming the school or teacher for the failing grade. While there are usually improvement strategies schools and teachers can implement to improve, I seldom leave these conversations with recommendations from the families on what strategies the students can use to improve themselves. Why would some families seek an "educational bail out?" As a principal, I did not understand it, but as a parent I can totally relate. When my child failed academically, it hurt. I remembered that Henry Ford once said, "Failure is simply the opportunity to begin again, this time more intelligently." But, considering this quote, why did this failure still hurt so much? I found the answer in psychology.

As Carol Dweck, author of *Mindset* says, there are two types of mindsets, "growth" and "fixed." A "fixed mindset" views failure as a name or a condition. "Fixed mindset" people are hurt by the failing. I was fixed about my daughter's grade. Dr. Dweck says, "In a growth mindset, challenges are exciting rather than threatening." So rather than thinking, "Oh, I'm going to reveal my weaknesses," you say, "Wow, here's a chance to grow." Sacrificing the long-term health of our children for the short-term boost in self-esteem doesn't work in the short-term either. The stress of maintaining high self-esteem in a society of consistent expectations to win, be the best, most liked and smartest is proving disastrous to our students. We can teach students to cope, but we must understand about the formation of high self-esteem. In order to have high self-esteem, a child must have a balance of emotional and cognitive self-esteems. Emotional self-esteem comes from the trophies, "A" grades, compliments, recognitions and "likes" on social media outlets, but these are short-term and usually dependent on others to give. The long-term and the most beneficial is the cognitive self-esteem. This only comes when a person has mastered skills through hard work. When they fail at a task, stick to the task in the face of adversity, problem solve how to overcome the obstacles and complete the task by themselves, the result is a boost in cognitive self-esteem.

It is this ability that Harvard Researchers have deemed the single most important trait of successful people (Moffitt, 2011). As a result, I want my students and my children to F.A.I.L. well. I want them to Face Adversity In Life and overcome adversity by learning from their mistakes and improving their skills. What does this mean for practice? We must EMPOWER students to overcome adversity.

For Schools: If a student fails an assignment, we must create the structures and practices to allow that student to keep working at that assignment until there is an improvement towards proficiency. This will foster a growth mindset in the student and boost the cognitive self-esteem. We cannot allow a student to fail and move on without providing an opportunity to overcome the difficulties. Too many adults claim, "I'm not good at math" because they never learned how to conquer or overcome adversity in mathematics at some point in their schooling.

For Students: Don't let them seek the "BAIL OUT." Instead, strengthen their cognitive self-esteem by focusing on the process for growth. When students are empowered to improve their own academic conditions through perseverance, patience and problem-solving, they will meet the high expectations we have set for them. Let students Face Adversity in Life and Win. Failure is not just a word; it's an opportunity to learn and practice an urgently needed lesson that will help students throughout their lives.

Empowered by the Process

My second third-grade teacher, Mrs. Shivers, believed in empowering me to overcome adversity. Her favorite words were, "Do it again." Even when the rest of the class moved on to new material, she would require that I stay on the lesson that I did not master and "Do it again." I had to redo and redo the assignment until I mastered it. She was uncompromised in her expectation. Each time I did the work it would improve. Mrs. Shivers gave no bail outs. She gave hope. For the first time in my young schooling career, I started to feel confident in my academic abilities. My rate of academic growth was astounding to my teacher, mother and especially to me. I went from straight "F's" in the 3rd grade to winning two city-wide essay contests by the end of the 6th grade.

I am deeply troubled when I think about the statistical predictability that students who fail the 3rd grade will eventually go on to drop out of school. I credit Mrs. Shivers for saving my life, though I never told her how much she meant to me. I did not appreciate it at the time, but she believed in my ability and held me accountable until I started believing in myself.

My mother heard me tell the Mrs. Shivers' story at an award ceremony when I was named the 2018 Outstanding Black Alumnus for the University of South Carolina. On the way home she provided some context I never considered. My mom said she had never heard me tell that story. Had she heard my account of the events, she would have corrected me. "You were always a gifted child," she said. I reminded her of the all "F's" report card that I tried to doctor into an all "A's" report card. "Would a gifted child have tried to do that?" I responded. Then she replied, "Your father and I got divorced that year and you took it pretty tough. We moved to DC after the school year started and you struggled with the adjustment." She explained that I would work at all the assignments at home and complete them, but at school, I would shut down and not put forth any effort. Mrs. Shivers would not allow me to shut down. She expected that her students would be empowered to maximize their full potential. Each time I had to "Do it again," I learned about the power of the process. In short, Mrs. Shivers realized that it was not the amount of material students mastered that made them successful, it was the ability to learn how to fail and how to cope that made the difference.

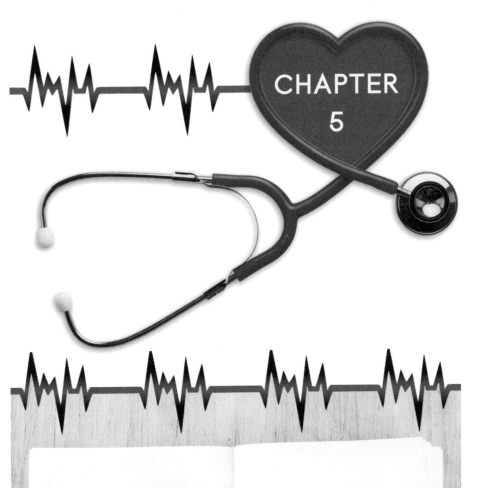

SHIFTING OUR MEASUREMENT MINDSET

> This power can defeat the Storm,
>
> It can remove the clouds of doubt,
>
> This Power grows with Faith works,
>
> Measured by quality inside not out.

"What does failure mean to you?" This was the second question I asked of students in the senior interviews. Like the "Who are you?" question outlined in Chapter 2, the failure question was also difficult for students to answer. I could tell because of the hesitation with their responses. In an environment where failure is a bad condition, I wanted to know how they conceptualized a condition that they would face in their lives. The seniors I interviewed understood failure as either a bad thing that needs to be avoided or they saw failure as good because it taught lessons that would allow them to grow. Regardless of how they viewed failure, I would tell them why Colonel Sanders' definition of failure serves as an inspiration for us all.

In his 2012 book, *Colonel Sanders & the American Dream*, author Josh Ozersky gives an amazing account of the obstacles one man faced and overcame to be a success. At one time, the image of Colonel Sanders was the most recognized brand in the world. Most of my students had no idea that Colonel Sanders of Kentucky Fried Chicken, now KFC, was a real man. I explained to them that Colonel Sanders was not a military colonel but a Kentucky Colonel, which is an honor bestowed to citizens who have made amazing contributions to the state. He was born Harland Sanders in Henryville, Indiana. His father passed when Harland was young and he was left to care for his younger siblings. Harland learned how to cook out of necessity. He was responsible for supporting the household while his mother worked. A very interesting part of the Colonel Sanders story is how much failure he faced in his life. He had many jobs/careers. He drove a trolley, was a lawyer, served as a secretary, and tried sales. He sold products as diverse as insurance, lamps and tires. All these careers had no successful future for him. When he realized that his retirement check would not be enough to support him, he decided to keep working. So at the age of 65, Harland Sanders opened Sanders Café in Corbin, Kentucky. This was a fueling station with a café attached. Drawing on his cooking skills, he created his famous "11 herbs and spices" recipe. Patrons at his café encouraged him to expand because he had a winning formula that was exceptionally delicious and unique.

The core of Harland Sanders' inspiration came from his quest to find a partner. He would drive to a restaurant or the home of a potential investor, cook up a batch of his chicken and ask for partnership. He went to the first investor and was told "no." I asked the students how many times Sanders was denied before he received his first "yes." Their answers ranged between 10 times to 20 times. I doubled their number and informed them that after 40 straight "no's" Sanders persisted. After 100 straight "no's," he persisted. After 500 straight "no's," he persisted. Playing up the suspense I asked the seniors, "Would you persist with your goal after 500 consecutive failures?" They all admitted that they would not. After 800 "no's" and 900 "no's" Harland Sanders continued to believe in his idea and persisted through 1009 consecutive failures until he received a "Yes!" What was failure to Colonel Sanders? The answer was giving up on his dream. Colonel Sanders dropped out of school because he believed he could not pass Algebra, yet he was able to learn that failure meant to keep learning.

The Standard Problem

The main obstacle holding and impeding many students from maximizing their potential in school is the requirement that all students have to be taught all academic standards. Challenging the standards is educational blasphemy to most educators because academic standards are sacrosanct to professional educators. Teachers are given curriculum guides that help them pace through the material. The objectives of each lesson derives from the state standards. These standards are developed by teachers and administrators and represent what a child should be able to do by a particular time in their educational career. The major assumption is that each year's learning will build on the next year. Therefore, a student in the 12th grade has mastered at least 60% of the standards presented to them. To hold schools accountable, students are tested on an undisclosed amount of state standards to ensure teachers are covering the material. I taught in a high poverty, high minority public school in an urban setting. I served as principal in a low poverty, majority white public school in a suburban setting. These schools are totally opposite on many characteristics. The most glaring commonality in all schools is the fact there is no such thing as a "standard student."

In "Education 101," future educators learn about the bell curve. This curve represents the distribution of performance that would result if a large population were assessed or measured. For example, if you asked 1000 people their weight, height, income, and square footage of their home, you would receive a distribution of results that would resemble a bell when plotted on the X and Y axis. The X axis would represent the variable being assessed and the Y axis would be the units of measurement. Each chart would have a large distribution where most people would perform.

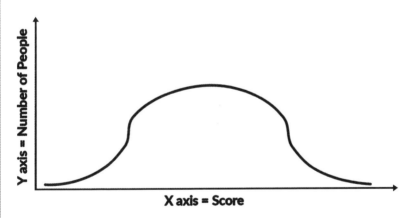

Additionally, there would be outliers. These outliers would represent the highest measurement(s) and the lowest measurement(s) of each variable. Of the total number of people assessed, there were typically more people who did not have the standard score even though it was the most common score. Subsequently, decisions about what to teach and assess mainly come from the common score. Even when schools divide the bell in an effort to make the standards more attainable and relevant, they merely create smaller bells curves.

As described in Chapter 2, the number of standards expected to be covered in a US History course is unrealistic. I decided to review all the standards a 9th grader in my high school would be responsible for learning during one calendar year. Nationwide, school systems are held responsible for graduating students 4 years after entering the 9th grade (McFarland 2018). I started by examining the academic expectations for these freshman. I was ashamed that I did not know all the standards, indicators and objectives that my students were required to learn. I do not think I was alone in this ignorance because I could not find anyone who could give me the total number of standards a freshman in high school was responsible for learning. So I decided to read all the state standards for English, Algebra 1, social studies, and science because failure in any one of these subjects means the student is at-risk of not graduating on-time. I found that students were expected to learn an average of 45 standards per subject. Some courses were as high as

There is no time for failure because we are teaching standards to children, not teaching children the standards.

50 standards. A freshman in my high school had to learn an average of 45 standards in four different courses. That's 180 standards! The school year is 180 days. That means students must master a standard each day. At this pace they cannot be absent for any time. It dawned on me that the problem compounds itself because students have more than four classes a year. Due to testing and school events, teachers are not given all 180 days of instruction. Students cannot fail and learn from their mistakes at this pace. There is no time for failure because we are teaching standards to children, not teaching children the standards. This is the "standard problem."

This is the "standard problem."

Metrics That Matter

It is difficult to determine the exact standard each student is ready to learn. At the heart of most equity issues in the school system is the notion that holding schools accountable for student achievement means that every school receive the same test. Even though there are no standard communities, no standard households, and no standard children, school accountability remains focused on testing the standard. In fact, accountability policy is based on what is easy to measure and not the metrics that matter the most. For example, my last year as a principal my school received 80% of its overall rating from three measures: English scores (25%), Math scores (25%) and the graduation rate (30%). Any principal or school administrator faced with this evaluation system would put a major emphasis on these three areas. While English and math scores ebbed and flowed with minimal gain over the years, graduation rates in my state as well as in the nation began to soar. A report from the South Carolina Department of Education in 2017, illustrated the growth in high school graduates from the 2009-2010 school year to the 2015-2016 school year jumped over 10%.

In the same year, the Commission on Higher Education released a report on the number of students entering post-secondary institutions, such as the military, technical schools and 4 year colleges and universities. This report showed that these rates have fallen 7% during the past 10 years.

Metrics That Matter

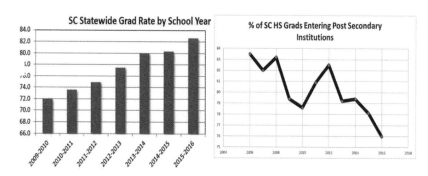

Source: SC Department of Education, 2017   Source: SC Commission on Higher Education, 2017

The over-focus on graduation rate is a poor metric of success if a growing number of high school graduates are not able to successfully enter post-secondary institutions. I am not an advocate for all students entering a four-year institution after high school, but I do advise students, not formally trained in a trade or skill in high school, to seek advance training in some post-secondary institution. Students with post-secondary degrees and certificates have higher lifetime earnings than students without them. According to a 2015 report by The Chronicle of Higher Education entitled College Completion, only 33.3% of students in U.S. colleges and universities can finish in 4 years ("College Completion," 2015). The study reports college graduation rates in terms of 150% time, meaning 57.6% of college students graduate in 6 years. There are a lot of reasons students do not complete their post-secondary studies. However, if only 1/3 of the students are able to accomplish their goal of graduating college on time, then there is a larger problem. This phenomenon affects all of us. Education is the fuel for the economic engine of our community, but only if the students are prepared.

From Graduation Rate to Preparation Rate

The true measure of success is not whether the student graduates on time. We should ask, "Is the student prepared on time?" Preparation rate is difficult to measure. It takes innovative leadership to go against the flow. Guy Kawassaki, a marketing specialist, became famous when he worked with Steve Jobs to market the Macintosh computer.

He tells an interesting story about the ice industry. The ice industry began when ice traders traveled out to the frozen lakes, cut large chunks of ice and loaded the large blocks on carts to be sold in the town. As time progressed, the ice factory was invented and the ice industry changed. No longer did the ice trader need to trudge to the frozen lake to cut ice. Ice could be delivered from a central location in any town and in any climate. Finally, the ice trader created a refrigerator. Now, the customer can make ice conveniently from home.

It is important to note the evolution in the ice industry caused the ice trader to go out of business each time there was a shift in the ice-making methodology. When the ice trader on the frozen lake was confronted with the idea of transitioning to centralized ice factories, he/she refused to innovate, choosing to continue what has worked in the past. When the ice factory owner was confronted with the possibility of making refrigerators, he/she refused to innovate, choosing instead to continue what has worked in the past. What will the refrigerator factory owner do when confronted by the next shift? If the leader has the ability to innovate to meet the customers' needs, then the organization will be successful. Guy Kawassaki calls this concept "curve jumping." The ability to jump to the next innovation is directly tied to the ability of leaders to focus on the vision of their organization. It is easy to get so focused on the mission of the organization because it's how things have been done for a long period of time. However, the mission of how we do our work should never block our vision- of why we do our work.

In chapter 2, I explained how my faculty and staff created a shared vision to prepare all students for productive lives. Improving the preparation rate for our students will require educators to jump the next instructional curve. Of all the innovative ideas I had as an educator, our Evening Acceleration Program had the greatest impact. Large numbers of students in Algebra were struggling with the concept of slope (rise/run) of a line and could not solve speed (distance/time) problems in science class because they did not understand fractions. Failing to understand fractions was causing a domino effect of failure in future assignments. When I asked why we aren't teaching fractions, one teacher answered, "It's not in the standards." Instead of focusing on the number of standards we teach, we should be focusing on what standards we need to teach. That was the vision of our Evening Acceleration School (EAS). Teachers recommended students with skill deficiencies. I paid Advanced Placement students minimum wage to work as tutors with their peers on these prerequisite skills. I was very impressed with the academic growth of the students. A major contributing factor to our school's academic growth, including a 16% gain in African American achievement, is this program's emphasis on giving students the prescribed standards, not merely the assigned standards.

I went back to my office and re-read the standards for all subjects and found that there were four words that kept recurring in the objectives and indicators of each standard in each discipline. The most frequently used words were (1) **understand**, (2) **analyze**, (3) **demonstrate** and (4) **develop.**

In his book, *Focus*, Mike Schmoker gives educators permission to simplify the mission of the school with a concept he calls, "Authentic Literacy- teaching the essentials." He found that students perform much better on achievement tests when their literacy skills are prioritized. Imagine if school personnel spent 180 days teaching students how to do those four literacy skills. Schools would not need to concern themselves with test scores because students who are proficient in the skills of understanding, analyzing, demonstrating and developing would be prepared for any test in life.

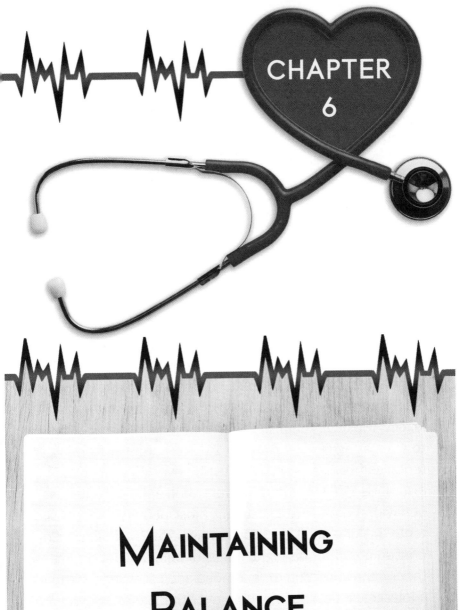

MAINTAINING
BALANCE

Let your Light shine, but not for credit of men,

Light nurtures the seeds of faith, the Spirit within.

For Heaven doesn't recognize the size of the tree,

It rejoices from the fruit on each branch we see.

When does a child become an adult? There is a temptation to answer this question in units of time. As early as 15 years of age, a person can receive a driver's permit. At the age of 17, a student is no longer required by law to attend school. At the age of 18, a citizen can vote in elections. At the age of 21, a person can consume alcohol legally. Most car rental agencies do not consider adulthood to start at ages 15, 17, 18 or 21. To rent a car from most rental companies, a person must be over 25 years old. The insurance industry which covers the rental vehicles uses behavioral data to suggest that most people start consistently making adult decisions at age 25. Psychologist Erik Erikson noted for his eight stages of personal development theory, the condition of "extended adolescence." Extended adolescence describes people over the age of 18 who are dependent and/or participate in risky behaviors. We can conclude, therefore, that time is a poor metric for determining when a child becomes an adult.

The adolescence period of human development provides physical indications that a person is nearing the adulthood status. The hormone changes are evident in the person's voice, the body as well as the behaviors. Yet, these changes do not signal when the person has become an adult. An adult is someone who is responsible. Adults can make logical decisions that consider logical long-term future outcomes. Most adults ask themselves, "How might my actions in the present affect me in the future?"

An analysis of decisions made by leaders was examined in the book, *That Used to Be Us* by Thomas Friedman and Michael Mandelbaum. The authors contend there are only two types of decisions a person can make. There are situational decisions and sustainable decisions. They argue that throughout the history of the United States there were leaders in place who made decisions that were based on what would be best for the nation in the future and sacrificed what would be best in the present. Taking the long view showed an adult level of responsibility and therefore qualified them as adults. To illustrate this point, an adult will save money, while a child decides to spend money. An adult will pay for needs first, a child will pay for wants first. An adult will plan for the future, while a child will plan day-by-day. The adult is constantly worried about the sustainability of the house, car, job, health, education, and retirement; while the child worries about the current conditions of the house, car, job, health and education. So, when does a person make the transition from thinking situationally to thinking sustainably?

Taking Off the Training Wheels

My children gave me the answer. My daughter is 4 years older than my son. I have learned a lot of lessons about teaching and learning from them. They have tested my theories of child development and discipline and sent me back to the drawing board to refine and revise my approach. I learned the most about child development when I gave my children their first two-wheeled bikes. The bike given to my daughter was accompanied with training wheels. After a year of riding with these extra wheels, I felt it was time for me to take them off. But she was not ready. Her fear of riding without the training wheels was so great and my patience with helping her overcome her fears was so low that I decided to keep the training wheels on. It was not until she saw the neighbor's child who was the same age riding on two wheels that she came to me and asked me to remove hers. Her willingness to learn how to peddle, brake and ride increased dramatically. Almost instantly she was off riding on two wheels with her friend. As a result, when it was time to teach my son how to ride his bike without training wheels, I thought I would just wait until the neighbor's children started riding their bikes and he would be willing to learn just like his sister. The only problem with this plan was that my son was the youngest child in our small neighborhood. There was no child his age or younger riding a bike on two wheels to serve as a model for him. As a result, he was very comfortable riding on the training wheels while the older children rode on two wheels. I began to ask the question, "At what age should a child have their training wheels removed?" Just as his sister did before she was motivated to learn, my son resisted my teaching. Unfortunately, his resistance persisted.

Like most parents today, I consulted the internet to find what age children were best able to learn to ride a bike and what are the effective strategies for teaching a child to ride. I thought the search would say that the optimal time was about the age of six – a year in the future and he would be ready. If that were the case, I would have an excuse for my ineffective teaching, and I would allow time to fix this issue. On the contrary, I found a parent blog on the subject and the consensus was that training wheels are most often used incorrectly.

The purpose of the training wheels is to teach the child how to balance by giving constant feedback about their ability to manage the forces that keep them unbalanced. Without going into the physics of angular momentum, the bike is balanced when the rider aligns the motion of both wheels. The more a rider practices this alignment the better he or she will be able to balance. The training wheels of my son's bike prohibited him from learning how to align the motion of the two main wheels. He always had four wheels on the ground and never had to balance. It was not until I lifted the training wheels from the ground that he was able to learn how to balance himself.

Such is the case for becoming an adult. There is no magic age when adulthood begins. Becoming an adult is dependent on the ability to align the "two wheels" in life. When people balance their desire to make situational decisions with their need to make sustainable decisions, then they are considered adults. Learning to ride a bike or learning to become an adult, depends on a person's ability to balance responsibilities. A person with no responsibilities will never be responsive. When my son was held responsible for balancing, he learned how to ride his bike.

Life Seeks Balance

I used to think that life was about seeking perfection. As a result, I tried to make my school, my children, my home and my marriage perfect. This became overwhelming and stressful. I could not manage all the requirements of being perfect. I finally gave up the pursuit of perfection. Believing that all of life's problems have already been solved by God's Law, I looked to Mother Nature for answers. In the natural world, life seeks balance not perfection. A study of any ecosystem will show the balance in the plant and animal life cycles perfectly adapts to the climate of that system. When these elements are aligned, the ecosystem thrives. This is not perfection; it is balance. Being balanced does not happen by accident. It takes work to achieve balance and work to maintain it.

The work of a child is the chief concern of parents and school personnel. As Carter G. Woodson stated in *The Mis-education of the Negro,* "The only way to elevate a person is to help them help themselves." It was a teacher who taught me about the principles of work. During a classroom observation, I stood in the back of the science teacher's classroom. With my note pad in hand, I began to take note of the actions of the teacher and the students. My observations would focus on the objectives of the class, the actions of the teacher and the actions of the students. These classroom visits were designed to assess the balance in the classroom ecosystem.

In the middle of my notes, I became caught-up in the topic of the class. As a rule, my teacher observations centered around the actions of the teachers and students in relationship to the objective for the day. I did not know all the standards and topics taught in my school. As a result, I was rarely in position to coach, critique or comment about the subject matter. On this day, it was the subject matter that gripped my full attention. The class objective required students to explain and apply the concepts of potential and kinetic energy. I had heard of these terms many times, yet it was the way this teacher explained the terms that captured my full attention. "Energy is the ability to do work." she told the class. I never made that connection. I had always understood energy in terms of electricity or gasoline, but I never made the connection to the definition that energy is work capacity. As she carried out her lesson plan, I found myself lost in my thoughts about work and energy. I had a lot of work to do and very little energy to do it. The unanswered emails, unreturned phone calls, the unchecked items on my to-do list, the meetings scheduled and unscheduled were dominating my mind. Prior to coming into this teacher's classroom, I was wondering where I was going to find the energy to do all this work. So when the teacher began to discuss the relation between energy and work, she had my full attention. I was particularly motivated to pay close attention to this teacher's lesson.

This science teacher's room setup was a traditional square classroom with a SMART board and white board at the front of the room. Instead of seats in rows facing the front of the room, her seats had their backs to the sides of the classroom. The students sat in three columns of five rows on each side of the class. I called this the "battle field" configuration because of the columns of students facing the other column looks like two ancient armies marching towards each other. The arrangement of desks created a large corridor in the middle of the class that would allow the teacher to walk from the front of the class to the back of the class. "Energy is the ability to do work" appeared on the SMART board and under this statement was a picture of a man with an arrow in full draw of the bow. My attention snapped back to the teacher as she talked, not because what she said next was loud or even particularly interesting. It was because she signaled key points in her discussion by bouncing a tennis ball that she held in her hand. The bouncing of the ball was not constant or rhythmic. It was sporadic. She bounced the ball before calling on a student to answer a question. Next, she bounced the ball before making a statement that students should record in their notes. She sometimes bounced the ball just to bounce the ball. I admired this technique. Like a playful terrier, I tracked that ball with my eyes and head everywhere it went and so did her students. Again, she bounced that ball and asked, "Can energy be created? Explain your answer."

The Potential to Do Work

I knew the answer to this question. I live five miles away from the Lake Murray Dam in Irmo, South Carolina. At the time of its completion in 1930, this dam was the largest earthen dam in the world. Impounding the Saluda River, this dam created Lake Murray, which was once the largest man-made lake in the world. Lake Murray and its dam have since lost this title of "World's Largest." The South Carolina Electric & Gas Company built the dam to operate a coal fire hydroelectricity power plant. I am reminded of where my energy comes from every morning when the trains blast their horns to signal their approach to the plant to unload tons of coal. I have even taken students to tour the McMeekin Power Plant behind the dam to see how the electricity is produced. The highlight of the trip was seeing students look into the larger boilers through a see-through thermal plate.

"Of course, energy can be created," I thought to myself. I am glad I thought to myself. A young lady raised her hand. When called on she stated confidently, "Energy cannot be created or destroyed." I turned my attention back to the teacher to see how she would respond to such a confident and wrong answer. "Correct!" the teacher exclaimed. "It's obvious you did your reading." I was confused. If she was correct, then what in the world was going on at the power plant? It certainly looked like they were creating energy to me. A student who must not have done the reading asked, "If power cannot be created then where does it come from when you do not have any?" I smiled at that young man for asking that question because I debated asking the question myself. At this point I was so captivated by the lesson, I stopped taking observation notes. She bounced the ball once. There were two sounds. The sound of the ball hitting the floor and the sound of the ball returning to her hand, "Boom-Tock." As soon as the ball returned to her hand, she asked, "Who can answer his question? If power cannot be created, then where does it come from?" Great teachers question students more than they tell students. This was a great teacher. "Energy is converted," a young man called out. "You are correct," she said. "Energy is stored or transformed." I am tuned in to every word of this discussion. The hydroelectric power plant in my town converts flowing water and fuel into electricity. I knew that the coal fed the fire in the boilers which heated the water to create steam which turned the turbines which subsequently produced electricity. It was in this teacher's class that I realized that the ability to do work or produce energy and power is stored up and waiting to be transformed.

Boom-Tock! She bounced the ball again. When the ball returned to her hand, she raised it out towards the class and she asked, "What kind of energy does this ball have right now?" There was a moment of silence. The silence continued. This was a great teacher because she did not end the silence by answering her own question. "Think class," she said. "If energy cannot be created or destroyed only stored and transferred, then what kind of energy does this ball have now?" As she paced back and forth through the center aisle, I could hear the pages of the text book turning. Finally, a student yelled out excitedly, "It has potential energy!" Potential energy is the stored energy or energy held up in an object. As an educator, I think about all the students who have so much potential and never produce any work. The natural law of potential energy can be applied to these students. Just as changing the position of the ball changes the potential energy of the ball, you can increase the potential energy of a person by changing his or her position. By changing the position of the ball such as raising it higher, you can increase the potential energy in that ball. If dropped, it will hit the floor faster and harder. Likewise, you can change the potential energy in students by changing their positions. For example, you can place them in tutoring classes, academic camps, reading interventions, honor classes and in arts to increase a child's potential energy, but that does not guarantee they will do work. So when she asked the next question, I was glad. I had overstayed the time I allotted for a classroom visit and stopped taking observation notes. I was learning so much, I did not want to leave.

"How do you convert potential energy into kinetic energy, the energy of work?" This was the question I was waiting on. Within the answer to this question was the secret to transforming the students with potential into students of work. She raised her arm up, extending the ball high in the air, then she released it. The ball fell to the ground. "Boom-Tock." When she caught the ball, she asked the students to explain using science vocabulary what happened to the ball that turned stored energy into work. Just then, my cell phone buzzed. I was needed elsewhere and I had to leave. For the rest of the day, I am thinking about the answer to the question.

When I arrived home, I noticed my children's bikes in the garage as I turned into the driveway. "Boom-Tock." The sound of the bouncing ball was still in my head. It dawned on me. My children on their bikes, just like the teacher's ball, were able to convert potential energy into work when released from the hand. I held the bike with my hands as they learned to ride, but my hand was doing the work for them. When I made the sustainable decision to release my grip and allow them to do the work, then they were able to achieve balance on their own. If a child is capable of performing a task, then no parent, teacher, or coach should do for that child what the child can do on their own.

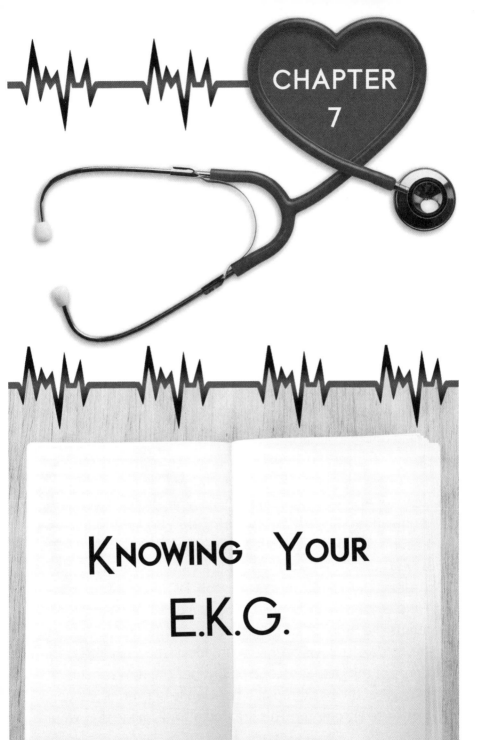

KNOWING YOUR E.K.G.

> The greatest Teacher seeks your Heart,
>
> And directs you toward your gift,
>
> So be an inspiration for others,
>
> Use your life to serve and uplift.

"Dr. Ross, are you okay?" asked my assistant. I was not okay. I never felt like this before. One moment I was standing in front of the school's support staff for our monthly scheduled meeting and the next moment I was leaning over a table in the front of the conference room where the staff had gathered. I was holding my chest. I could not take a full breath. When I heard her call for Emergency Medical Services (EMS), I knew this was serious. "This can't be a heart attack," I said to myself. I was not even 40 years of age. It was not until I was riding in the back of the ambulance with the sirens blaring that I realized I was not in control. I thought about my grandfather who had died of a heart attack. Edward Ross was an artist for a major news station, WTOP TV in Washington DC during the 1960s. He died of a heart attack at the age of 55. My family talks about the amount of stress he was under in his work. In those days, television news broadcast had painted backdrops of the city landscape or skyline. The news anchor sat in front of the backdrop at a desk while delivering the news from a teleprompter. This created a total image that would capture the attention of the viewer. Today, green screens and video displays can create in minutes what took weeks to create during the time of my grandfather's career. As an artist, he experienced continually high stress levels as he struggled with the deadlines required by the news station. This stress eventually damaged his heart to the point that it took his life. As I was hooked up to the EKG machine, the nurse asked me about the history of heart disease in my family. Not only had my grandfather died of a heart attack, but also his younger brother, my uncle, sustained a heart attack in his 40's. It did not take his life but changed it forever. I clearly was at-risk of heart disease and a full battery of tests were ordered to determine the health of my heart.

As I lay in the emergency room with monitoring pads all over my body, I will never forget the look on my son's face as he entered the hospital room where I was admitted. It was like he did not recognize the man laying there as his father. He did not speak to me, look at me or even give me one of those father-son hugs. When my wife left the emergency room to go pick up my daughter, I was left alone to think about how I had lost control of the health of my heart. I concluded and hopefully not too late that I was trying to do too much. I was seeking perfection in a world that rewards balance. Instead of my hands being in the work, I needed to learn how to better empower others to help do the work themselves. Alfred Adler, the great psychotherapist, teacher of Abraham Maslow and colleague of Sigmund Freud, argued that the role of the educator was to remove difficulties from the child and gradually put them into the position to solve problems on their own (Adler, Ansbacher

& Ansbacher, 1965). I became acutely aware that frightful day in the hospital that as an educator, empowering others heals and preserves the heart!

Empowered People, Empower People

In Chapter 3, I retold the story of the Tin Man in the *Wizard of Oz* series by L. Frank Baum. In that story we learned that of the three characters that Dorothy meets on the Yellow Brick Road only one had been human. The Tin Man was at one time a real man who sacrificed his human form for a mechanical form because he saw value in how much he could produce. His value was measured by his impact on material things not on people. When you think about the three characters and their needs from the Oz, its easy to draw parallels to the needs of all people. The Scarecrow needed a brain, so he represented the mind. The Cowardly Lion needed courage, he represented the strength of the body, and the Tin Man represented the spirit. What did the Tin Man need? When I ask this question, the response is almost always, "A heart." The reality was he did not need a heart. He needed two things. The first thing he needed was oil. When Dorothy met him along the Yellow Brick Road he was rusted and could not move. The oil reduced the friction and resistance to his movements. The oil was necessary to allow him to do work.

I think about a lot of our students who have the potential to do amazing work, but their energy is being bound up by the friction of emotional distress like anxiety, depression and substance abuse. These students also face the resistance of societal factors, such as poverty, racism, classism, disparities in housing, education and health care. These students have amazing potential, yet without the "oil" used to help them overcome the resistance and friction of life, they can never succeed. As educators we must be the "oil" for our students. We must break the bounds of resistance that prohibit our students from maximizing their own potential. The work of school counselors, classroom teachers, social workers, community groups, administrators, parents and school staff must align to find, assess and eliminate the individual obstacles holding a student back. School reforms that target solely the academic deficiencies of the child without accounting for the social-emotional, financial, cultural, racial, medical and class deficiencies of a child will have marginal impacts at best. When barriers are removed from the lives of children, then their potential energy can be converted to work.

The second need of the Tin Man was related to the quality of his work. When the Tin Man finally reached the Great and Powerful Oz, he realized in his quest to defeat the Wicked Witch of the West that he already had a heart. He was able to show compassion and empathy for his friends; he was able to sacrifice his situational needs for the sustainable needs of the group. What he needed was a testimonial. The testimonial was acknowledgement that he mattered.

It's significance and purpose that heals the heart.

Educating the Heart

The needs of the Tin Man parallel greatly with the tenants of Individual Psychology. Adler felt that every person is in struggle over two forces: (1) the struggle over inferiority – the feeling that a person is less than others or of lower quality and (2) inadequacy – the extent to which people feel that they can control their environment. In his writings about *The Individual Child in School*, Alder writes:

> *An educator's most important task, one might say his holy duty, is to see to it that no child is discouraged at school, and that a child who enters school already discouraged regains his self-confidence through his school and his teacher. This goes hand-in-hand with the vocation of the educator, for education is possible only with the children who look hopefully and joyfully upon the future. (pg. 399-400)*

As a result of these key elements of a balanced and healthy life, I created a model for educators to serve as a tool for empowering students to maximize their potential.

Heart Empowerment Model

E.K.G.

Empowered = Knowing your gift/ Giving your gift

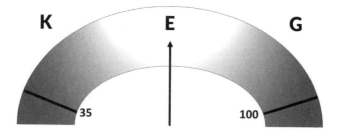

Just as the Automated External Defibrillator (AED) searched for the rhythm of the heart of the clinically dead man in the 1st chapter of this book, educators must search for the E.K.G. of the student. I call it the *Heart Empowerment Model*. The "E" stands for Empowered, meaning living a balanced and sustainable life. To be empowered, a person must align the need for "K" or Knowledge of your gifts or abilities, and "G" or Giving of your gifts to others.

Empowered = Knowing your Gift / Giving your gift

The rhythm of the heart can be determined from the pulse. A fast pulse symbolizes the quest to prove superiority in terms of production of money, achievement, and status. Productivity increases the heart rate. Cardiologists warn that a continual, long-lasting fast pulse over 100 beats per minute is dangerous for the heart and can lead to death. A pulse that is under 35 beats per minute is too slow and not healthy either.

The slow pulse is symptomatic of the person who is fighting to overcome inadequacy and inferiority. Their ability to find success within their environment causes them to drop out or withdraw from the process or the institution altogether. The low pulse person seeks any place of comfort to revive them. Cardiologists warn that the low pulse can also be as deadly. The ideal rhythm of the psychological heart is the empowered pulse. Just as the normal heartbeat rhythm signals the sustainable pumping of blood throughout the body, the Empowered Pulse is evidence of an optimal, joyful and balanced way of living.

We can ask two questions to determine if a person is empowered.

(1) Who are you? This question seeks to understand their feelings about inferiority. Students who know exactly who they are can think for themselves. They have identified their passions. When society tells them they are not good enough, smart enough, wealthy enough or beautiful enough, they can stare in the mirror and affirm their value and worth by making affirmation statements towards themselves.

(2) What is failure? This question seeks to understand a person's feelings about their purpose and power. In his last sermon at Ebenezer Baptist Church in Atlanta, Georgia, Dr. Martin Luther King Jr. gave his famous "Drum Major" Speech. Referencing Alfred Alder, Dr. King said we all have the need for attention and the desire to be first. He preached that we must use this instinct for the benefit of others. According to Dr. King, the joy of living is in the service of others (King, 1968). When students know who they are in the present, then they will understand their passions and gifts. The only time a person can experience the feeling of real joy is in the present and the only time a present can be enjoyed is when it is unwrapped to reveal the gift. Further, a person who sees failures as part of the path and process to empowerment will be more able to sustain through any failure.

As Best As You Can

The cardiologist ordered a battery of tests to fully understand the condition of my heart. The stress test was the toughest. I was asked to run timed intervals on a treadmill while numerous electrodes were attached to my chest. The cardiac nurse informed me that the longer I stayed on the treadmill the more reliable the results would be. It had been years since I ran on a treadmill. I had access to treadmills at the school and one at home, but I never used either. Too late now. I had to get on this machine and try to keep pace for as long as I could. Honestly, my stress levels were rising before the test even started.

The purpose of the stress test was to evaluate the blood flow to my heart to ascertain any evidence of heart disease. When I stepped on the treadmill, all I could think about was the fast food, candy and sodas I made part of my daily diet. As the test began, my anxiety subsided because the pace was easy. I could handle the pace with no problem. I was having small talk with the cardiac nurse asking about her family and her favorite sports team. Then she informed me that every three minutes the speed would increase and so would the incline. By the ninth minute, there was no small talk or talk at all from me. When the nurse asked me a question, I could only mumble an inaudible sound and pray she could translate that into English. At the 12 minute mark, I had enough! My body lost all resemblance of a runner. I was stumbling wildly all over that treadmill. I thought I had been running for an hour and was furious that the timer only said 12 minutes. As a former Division I college football player, I should have had a better stress test than 98% of the people tested. Mine felt like the worse. From the ninth minute to the twelfth minute, I was not even running. I was really preventing myself from falling.

That is exactly how I was living life. As the work load of the school sped up and the difficulty of my responsibilities became steeper, I was not living a balanced life. I was going from one issue to the next in an attempt to prevent myself from falling. The cardiologist concluded that I did not have a heart attack, but instead a panic attack. He advised that I get my stress under control by living balanced. The E.K.G. model serves as my guide for living a balanced life. I have committed myself to daily monitoring of my own E.K.G. As a result, I want students to be empowered to monitor and balance their E.K.G. Students who know their gifts and give their gifts are then empowered.

When was the last time you measured your E.K.G.?

How will you maintain balance?

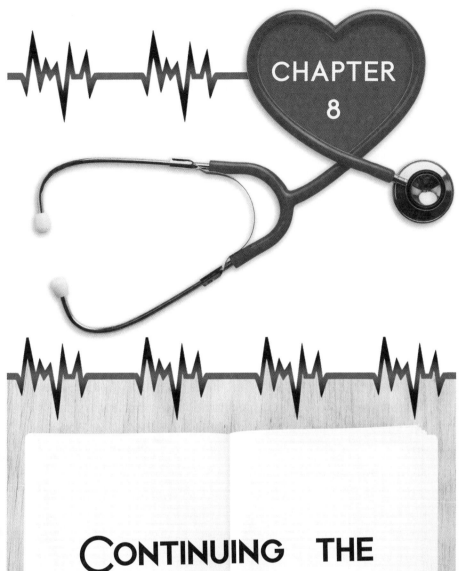

CONTINUING THE HEARTBEAT

> As we travel along life's journey,
>
> We will stumble and we will fall,
>
> Remember, Love conquers ALL Storms,
>
> Because the Heart EMPOWERS Us All.

The *Heart Empowerment Model* is not a stage model of psychological development. I do believe that a person journeys through multiple stages of development as described by great thinkers like Erik Erikson, Jean Piaget and Abraham Maslow. I assert that life is not static. Life requires us to constantly balance against the forces that can misalign our struggle for inferiority and inadequacy. The *Heart Empowerment Model* serves as a guide for living a fulfilled and joyous life and sustaining that joy through failures, obstacles and the storms of life. This has been my mission as an educator. I set upon the work of empowering students to be servant leaders of others, thus creating a society that sustains peace and love. Chapters 8 & 9 will outline how educators can put this model into practice in their schools and classrooms.

Empowering the Heart (System Model)

I believe that Mother Nature has a solution for each of life's problems. As a result, I created an empowering system that works very much like a human heart or any sustainable ecosystem. Energy is pumped from the source through the system allowing work to be done for each element of the system. The outcome of the system returns to the source as renewable fuel to continue the process again.

There are four elements of this model. These elements have been discussed at length in this book. Therefore, I am providing four guiding questions for the model that will help school personnel assess the health of their school system and provide a guide for removing resistance and obstacles to an otherwise optimally functioning system.

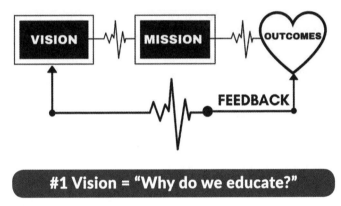

#1 Vision = "Why do we educate?"

The power source of any organization is the vision. This is the reason people join an organization. Failure to ensure that the vision is true to the passions of the employees will limit the amount of power flowing from the source. To maximize the power of the vision, educators should ask, "Why do we educate?" Asking this question of all the stakeholders of school will allow school leaders to establish a common vision that communicates the intended outcome. As described in Chapter 2, my school personnel chose to prepare ALL students for productive lives.

#2 Mission = "How do we educate?"

After you have established a common vision, the behaviors and attitudes needed to accomplish the vision must be aligned. The mission of the school must include the processes the educators use to accomplish the vision. Therefore, school personnel must ask themselves, "How do we educate?" It is important to note the use of the word 'processes' to describe the mission. There is no one perfect way to maximize the potential and prepare all students. Providing equitable educational opportunities for all students means school personnel should seek to remove the individual barriers that prohibit a student from being empowered. There are four domains of an effective school mission. The school mission must give students responsibilities (Chapter 3), measure what matters (Chapter 5), teach students to F.A.I.L. (Chapter 4), and remove the training wheels (Chapter 6). These domains are based on the psychological needs of a person. I call the four domains, "The Heart-Needs."

I call these four domains, the "Heart-Needs."

♡ Give students responsibilities

♡ Measure what matters

♡ Teach students to F.A.I.L.

♡ Remove the training wheels

Humans are social beings. Not only do we want to be part of a group, but we also seek significance within that group. This need for socialization is central to effective development. A school administrator asked me if I had any solutions for the "gang problem" at his school. I asked him, "Why do students join gangs?" "I never thought about why students join gangs," he responded. I said they join gangs for the same reason we joined a fraternity, a sorority, a civic or community organization or social order. They wear their gang colors and paraphernalia for the same reason we wear the colors and apparel of our alma mater. They seek acceptance in an organization that meets their needs of safety and purpose. They seek love and significance from a family group. If the street gang is the only option for the family structure, then there is a high likelihood schools will continue to have a "gang problem." Students will not drop out of organizations they feel connected to. I made every opportunity to provide all students a club or organization that focused on their passion. On the first day of school, I would bring the entire student body into the arena for one hour. This was my opportunity to teach our norms, beliefs and behaviors. It reminded me of the one room schoolhouse days. I had 1400 students in one space, and I had to keep their attention for 60 minutes.

My best strategy for engaging the students was The Heartbeat. I would say, "One Heartbeat, Ready!" and the students would respond with two claps. The sound of the collective claps of 1400 students sound like two strikes on a massive bass drum – "Boom Boom." You could feel the percussion of the Heartbeat. At one point in the assembly I would ask them to continue the Heartbeat. "Boom-Boom. Boom-Boom. Boom-Boom." It sounded and felt like the school building had come alive. Together, they created the embodiment of a living and thriving organization. Each student contributed to the Heartbeat and played a role in making the school their home away from home.

There is another reason for the Heartbeat. Not every student's pulse was at the optimal level. Some students arrived at school very stressed with fast heartbeats. Others barely made it to school and were on the verge of dropping out. However, musicians know that the drummer in the band controls the rhythm. The loudest beat draws all other beats to its pace. So, when 1400 students produce the thunderous cadence of "Boom-Boom. Boom-Boom. Boom-Boom," it has the effect of calming the stressed and motivating the depressed.

School personnel and curriculum leaders must examine the work we require of our students in terms of ability to ultimately prepare students for productive lives. On a recent trip to the United States Department of Education Summit on Rethinking Career and Technical Education (Rethink Schools 2018), the consensus from many businesses was that students needed more practical skills over classical knowledge. There is an imbalance of classical curricula in schools because school accountability systems can easily measure student achievement in metrics of content knowledge. What is tough to measure on a standardized test are literacy skills, collaboration, team work, integrity and perseverance. The skills that are difficult to assess on standardized tests are the required skills for success in life. As

I described in Chapter 5, I started an Evening Acceleration School to teach literacy skills to students. Evening Acceleration School was used to teach the most important skills and to use student-selected material and assignments to ensure mastery of the concepts. The growth rate from this after-school program was remarkable.

#3 Outcomes = "What did we produce?"

I devoted an entire chapter to this concept because of its importance in maintaining a balanced and purposeful life. School personnel could greatly benefit from the "growth mindset" research of Carol Dweck. Practices, language and attitudes around failure could help build a child's coping skills and resiliency abilities. In the fast pace world of standard grading, students who fail are asked to "move on" to the next topic. There is no time provided to improve. I am fortunate I had a teacher who taught me, "Good, better, best, never let it rest until your good is better and your better is best!" School personnel are obligated to examine the conceptualization of failure based on their practices. When the Vision and Mission are aligned, the outcome will equal the intent. School personnel must be courageous enough to ask, "What did we produce?" If the production question is answered by the metric graduation rate, then there will be a misalignment between the vision and the outcomes. This misalignment will weaken the system's empowerment ability. Instead, school personnel should use the preparation rate. It is very rewarding to work in a system where the effort educators put into their jobs matches the rewards they expect. We expect to prepare students for productive lives.

#4 Feedback = "Who are you?"

The last part of the model is as important as the source of the power. This is the feedback we receive from the students. I conducted senior interviews because I wanted to hear from the students themselves if they felt like we made a difference. I learned some of our practices were not making a positive difference in the lives of our children. The practice of student discipline was called into question. As principal, I took pride in my discipline tools. I levied detentions and suspensions on students who did not meet the behavioral expectations of the school. However, these tools were not effective with all students. I sought advice from my team because I was frustrated with the repeated offenses from students who received detentions and suspensions. It was a school counselor and special education teacher who showed me why my behavioral expectations were not being met. "Discipline means to teach. Punishment means to pay," they said. "If you want to see a change in their behavior, you must empower them to make the best decisions," added the Special Education teacher. When a student broke the rules, I confused punishment with discipline.

We decided to teach students the behaviors we wanted to see so we created the Haven, in our view, the best-looking detention hall in the Nation. The Haven had soft lighting, bean bags and a night skyline mural with glow in the dark stars, all accompanied by soft music. The frequent offenders of school rules were sent to the Haven with a counselor. The goal of the time in this space was to teach the appropriate behaviors and defuse and deescalate future incidents. I was amazed at how many students were not equipped with the behavioral tools to maintain self-control. In the first year, the Haven served 10 students. These 10 students were failing 50% or more of their classes and accumulated the most behavior referrals in the Freshman class. After a semester of intervention and empowering student-led conversations about their growth all but one student received a suspension and all students in the program were promoted to the 10th grade.

In the feedback phase of the system we ask, "Who are you?" The system would be refueled if the student replies something like, "Who I am is the gift in my heart; I will use my gift to serve others. I am strong enough to overcome all obstacles and withstand all the storms in life. I am able to have a balanced life because I am empowered."

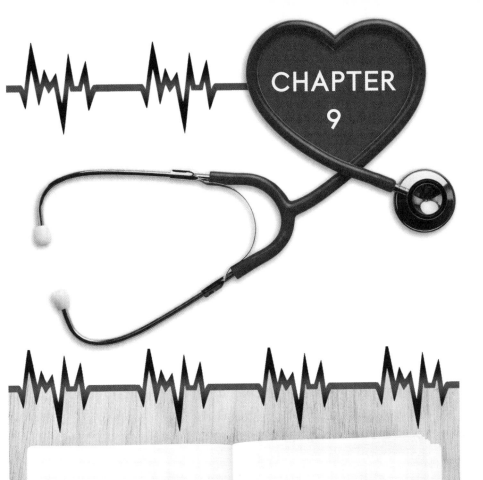

CHAPTER 9

EMPOWERED PEOPLE WILL EMPOWER PEOPLE

Empowering in the Real World

"Here we go again. Another initiative that we have to implement in addition to the other initiatives that we half-way implement." I overheard one teacher complain as he leaned over to his colleague. I could not decide if this comment was stated loud enough for me to hear or the teacher was a poor whisperer. Regardless, I rolled my eyes and dismissed the teacher's sentiment as a complaint from a disgruntled faculty member. Turning my attention back to the presenter, I adorned my best 'engaged face' as I pretended to take copious notes.

It was back to school time for teachers. Before the students returned to class, school personnel are given between three to five paid days to prepare for the first day of school. We called these Professional Development days, PD days for short. In reality, I never gave them all of that time. The majority of the professional development time was spent sitting in trainings. These required trainings in isolation are essential. Examples of these trainings are on safety, school policy, special education law, school operations, technology, social media, etc. When combined, these trainings dominated the allotted professional development time. As a result, the faculty and I would engage in a bitter silent battle over the remaining amount of time. My faculty and staff wanted to use this time for setting up their classes, making copies, planning with teacher colleagues, setting up labs, securing resources and becoming mentally prepared. I wanted to use that time to introduce, gain buy-in and implement new instructional initiatives. This conflict led to the tension in the Professional Development Room as the faculty sat through training for a new instructional initiative. This tension is an example of how the "real world" affects our plans. There are always powerful forces affecting the integrity of every initiative. Just as a ship at sea is tested by the forces of the wind and waves, so will any change initiative be tested by the forces of the "real world." The wise leader accounts for these forces and successfully navigates through the storm. I received my lesson in navigation at the most unexpected time.

A Lesson from Thanksgiving

There is a professional development cycle. It begins with the school administrator learning about a school improvement strategy in the summer, presenting this strategy schoolwide in the fall, trouble-shooting through implementation problems in the winter, prioritizing standardized testing over the school improvement strategies in the spring, and back to seeking new school improvement strategies in the summer. The powerful inertia of the professional development cycle was made evident to me before a Thanksgiving holiday.

By the end of November, the Back-to-School honeymoon period has ended. The excitement of starting the new school year with new students has been replaced by the mundane familiarity that comes when people spend most of their time together. This routine can have a negative effect on the morale of the school personnel. Low morale for the faculty is never good for the students. As principal, I thought the solution to improving morale was buying things for the staff. I received positive feedback from the purchase of shirts, jackets, and scarves for the school personnel. However, the best appreciation came when I provided food for the staff. Therefore, one year I planned a Thanksgiving luncheon to lift the spirits of the faculty and staff. The school leadership team had an idea of doing staff superlatives each month. The leadership team would create a fun inter-department contest. Each department was responsible for submitting an entry, which would be featured in the newsletter. The faculty and staff would vote for one department of which they were not a member. The department with the most votes was declared the winner. The school counseling department won October's Halloween costume contest. I wanted to win November's contest. The challenge for November was the dessert contest. Each department would submit an entry for the Thanksgiving Luncheon and the winner would be declared by a criterion of appearance and taste.

In my weekly administrators' meeting, one of the agenda items was the dessert entry for this faculty challenge. I must admit, it was the only topic of that meeting I was looking forward to discussing. When we arrived at said topic, I put pressure on the two administrators who had baking experience to create a winning entry. Their response was a simultaneous look of contempt which instantly turned this topic to my least favorite agenda item. "First of all, you didn't even ask us to bake," my assistant principal of instruction said as she turned to me. She continued, "Now you have the nerve to pressure us to bake a winning entry. How about you bake a winning entry?" The meeting was over at this point. She put down her pen, looked me in the eye and waited for my response. Just as I was about to turn my head, I heard, "Don't even think about looking at me!" said my assistant principal of operations (the only other member of my administrative team with baking experience). I had really messed up, but I could not back down from this challenge. So I doubled down and said confidently, "I will make a cake for the administration and it will be the winning entry." Their laughter made me doubt my ability to pull this off. It was open season on me as the administrative team joked about how I wrote a check that I could not cash, which is southern for I messed up. Determined to have the last laugh, I left the meeting and went to my office to begin my research (my instructional leadership was worthless for the remainder of the day). As I perused images of creative cakes on various baking websites, suddenly there it was! The perfect cake for this contest. The cake was featured on www.recipes.com and was shaped in the form of a school bus with yellow icing. The front of the cake had a blue window and black bumper. What sold me on this cake were the eyes and mouth added to the front of the bus. It was as if the school bus was alive.

The night before the school Thanksgiving luncheon, I drove to the grocery store and bought what I thought were the necessary ingredients. After putting my kids to bed, I began to assemble the ingredients on the kitchen countertop. The directions on the box gave me confidence that I would have a successful outcome. Combine, mix, pour and bake were the action steps. These directions seemed well within my scope of ability when I began at 8pm. By midnight, after a few failed attempts, my confidence turned into frustration. Simply putting the ingredients into the bowl and expecting them to combine into one was my first mistake. The substance that emerged from the oven could barely stand on its own much less be formed into a school bus. By 2am, my frustration turned into desperation. I went from trying to make a masterpiece to just being satisfied that the icing was able to stay on the cake and it was edible. When I arrived to school with this disaster of a dessert, I was met immediately by the assistant principal of instruction. "Let me see the winning entry," she said sarcastically. It was like she could see through the translucent cake platter with sharp definition. She began to laugh before I even unveiled the cake. By this time, the front office staff had gathered around to see firsthand my attempt to outperform people with superior skill and experience. When the audience had reached the standing capacity of the assistant principal's office, I removed the cover. The staff's reaction was so immediate to the unveiling of the cake that it sounded like I had an audio file of roaring laughter under the cake platter lid. The laughter brought some of the staff to tears. The flurry of questions about how a cake could come to such an unfortunate state were too many to answer. I just stood there helpless as people began to take cell phone pictures of me with this cake. It was at this point that I learned a very important lesson about leadership.

Every summer, school administrators find some new strategy, program or methodology that was proven to be successful in one setting and they try to implement it the exact way in their setting. The result of these quickly implemented school-wide improvement strategies is more disastrous than the cake I made. When the intent of the program does not match reality, leadership is compromised, school personnel is demoralized, and students are penalized. The success or failure of a program has little to do with the practitioner's knowledge about the initiative. Success is determined by the degree to which the practitioner applies the necessary skills to the task.

The teacher who made the "Here we go again," comment in our professional development was not disgruntled. He was correct. He understood the professional development cycle all too well and was powerless to stop it. The Thanksgiving lesson is a reminder to empower our people by providing them the tools and strengthening their skills in accomplishing their goals.

The Real World is Real

I draw a lot of inspiration from nature. God's perfect creation has the answers to all of our problems. Only when we still ourselves in the natural world will the solutions be revealed. The solutions for achieving our desired outcomes also come from the natural world. For example, no two people are exactly alike. Even identical twins have differences. Of all the human beings that have ever lived and will ever live, none of the fingerprint patterns will be exactly alike. This fact provides perfect guidance for school leadership. The real world is real and it must be accounted for in all change initiatives. No school-wide improvement strategy can be implemented exactly the same. As a behavioral scientist, the effective educator is chiefly concerned with the condition of the learner. He or she will remove barriers that interfere with the child's ability to learn. The behavioral scientists would apply their skills to school improvement. Viewing the school as an inanimate system will lead to an over reliance on processes, strategies and programs to achieve the goal. However, viewing the school as a living system will lead to a better understanding of the factors that interfere with school improvement. Schools are impacted by their environment. Therefore, any school improvement model, program, strategy or initiative must be viewed in context of the environmental forces that is acting on the system.

Figure 1 illustrates how the *empowerment system* is affected by its environment. Each arrow represents one environmental force affecting the success of the school improvement initiative. The environmental affect could be positive or negative. The positive forces improve the chances of accomplishing the intended outcomes. I have traveled across the United States and I have yet to find an under-performing school in a thriving community. Thriving school communities create thriving schools. Conversely, the negative forces diminish the chances of accomplishing the intended outcomes. In short, without considering the environmental forces acting on the school, school leaders will not fully understand why their school improvement initiatives succeed or fail.

Because each school has a unique array of environmental forces that act on it, the ability of school personnel to understand these forces and the degree to which they impact a school is imperative. The figure below is a framework that can be used to identify the variable forces associated with improving or diminishing school improvement efforts.

Figure 1

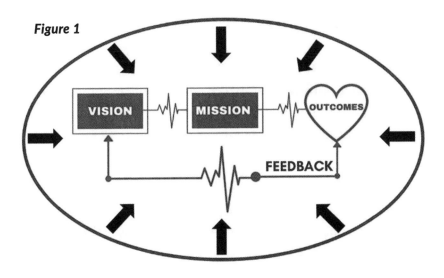

How Do We Take Off?

Improving school outcomes is analogous to the flight of a Boeing 747 Jumbo Jet. A tremendous amount of power is required to lift a fully loaded jumbo jet into the air. Being that I had access to his expertise, I asked the commander of my school's Navy Junior Reserve Officer Training Corps (NJROTC), Marine Colonel "Buddy" Slack, how much power is needed to lift a large plane off the ground. Colonel Slack is an accomplished pilot and he, along with NJROTC teacher, Senior Chief Cook, were responsible for one of the nation's best leadership programs. In my last 5 years as principal, their program had a cadet admitted to the US Naval Academy each year. The NJROTC Battalion won a National Championship and was National Runner-up during my principal tenure. Colonel Slack is a highly decorated Marine combat pilot. He was a Section Commander in Vietnam, Aerobatics Instructor, a Helicopter Squadron Commander and even served as Chief of Staff for the Assistant Secretary of the Navy. Prior to becoming an instructor at my high school, he was the professor of Naval Sciences at the University of South Carolina. Colonel Slack is a proven leader, and I sought his counsel often. Most of his lessons were in the context of his military experience as a pilot. As a result, I have come to view school improvement like flying a plane.

I learned a lot from the Colonel's successes, but it was his failures that impacted me the most. Colonel Slack shared that he was involved in a plane crash. The crash landing broke his back, leaving his arm temporarily paralyzed for weeks. In February of 1972, Buddy Slack was a First Lieutenant Flight Instructor at the Naval Air Base in Pensacola, Florida. He trained pilots in a Beechwood T-34 B fixed wing aircraft. This single turbine engine plane resembled a World War II combat plane. It had a long nose with an even longer canopy covering the cockpit. This plane was used to train pilots. As a result, it had two seats. The student sat in the front and the trainer was positioned in the rear seat. The clear canopy provided great visibility for the student pilot. On this particular day, conditions were perfect for flying. Clear skies meant great visibility. The student was given the controls and instructed to proceed with take-off.

Every pilot is taught the laws of flight. Flight is achieved when the forces of Lift and Thrust are greater than the forces of Weight and Drag. The student was well aware of the laws of flight. However, the student panicked as wind sheer changed the flight dynamics of the plane during take-off. The student failed to provide enough power as the aircraft entered the wind sheer and lost control of the plane. Using all of his strength, Colonel Slack fought the cockpit controls but the plane slammed nose first into the ground. "I did all I could do to save our lives. We were hurt badly, but we survived." As a result of that day, Colonel Slack learned that "any random error can be fatal." I learned that every take-off should be at full throttle. A leader must always be prepared for the unexpected and the uncontrollable forces of real life. Approach all things with 100% effort.

Full Throttle

I use the principles of aerodynamics to explain the variables that will allow school improvement to rise or fall. There are four forces acting on an aircraft in flight. These forces are thrust, drag, lift and weight. The airplane creates thrust through the power of the engines that push the airplane forward. As this plane increases speed, friction from the air increases resulting in a dragging force. This drag resists its forward movement. for the plane to move forward, the thrust must be greater than this drag. The wings of the plane also create a lift force. Interestingly, just having wings does not guarantee lift. The shape of the wing creates the lift as it travels through the air. Without going into the details of hydrodynamics and the Daniel Bernoulli's principle, only wings designed to create an airfoil (lower air pressure on top and higher pressure on the bottom) will create lift. Weight is an opposing force against lift. In order for the plane to rise off the ground, lift must be greater than weight.

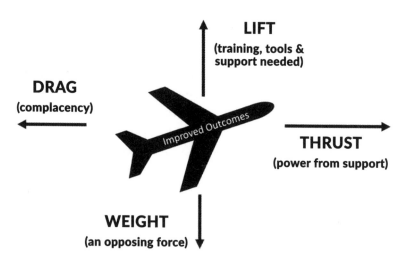

Thrust Over Drag. The Boeing 747 Jumbo Jet is 63 feet tall. When moving, this giant aircraft creates tremendous drag from the resistance of the air against the large surface area. As a result, the massive engines of the 747 jumbo jet must produce enough thrust to push the plane over 500 miles per hour.

The drag of school reform is complacency and comfort with the status quo. Leadership is required to engage and inspire school personnel and the school community in reform. The speed of the professional development cycle leads to administrators trading leading for managing school improvement. School leadership should ask themselves the following critical thrust questions:

> - **What percentage of my faculty and staff support the school improvement effort? Why?**

> - **What percentage of my students support the school improvement effort? Why?**

> - **What percentage of my community support the school improvement effort? Why?**

> - **For those who do not support or are complacent about the school improvement efforts, how do I address this?**

In his book *Leading Change*, Harvard Business School professor John P. Kotter gives reformers guidance on just how much power is needed to be transformational. "Sustaining a transformation effort in stages 7 and 8 demands an even greater commitment. A majority of employees, perhaps 75 percent of management overall, and virtually all of the top executives need to believe that considerable change is absolutely essential" (1996). Therefore, if 75 percent or more of the school personnel, students and community members support the school improvement efforts, then the efforts will move forward.

Lift Over Weight. The Boeing 747 Jumbo Jet has a gross weight over 800,000 lbs. Therefore, the lift needed to put 400 tons in the air is analogous to the power needed to achieve success in school improvement efforts. The shape of the wings is engineered to allow air to move faster over the top of the wing and move slower under the wings. This contrast of air speed around the wing causes a low pressure on top of the wing and higher pressure underneath. As it is with getting a school improvement effort off the ground, the amount of training, tools and support needed to lift the reform must outweigh the forces that work against student achievement. School leadership should ask themselves the following critical lift questions:

➢ **Does the school have financial support to implement the school improvement efforts?**

➢ **What skills will be required to implement the school improvement efforts by the school personnel?**

➢ **What is required in the community to support the school improvement efforts? Will the school have access to these community resources?**

➢ **What is required to support students in the school improvement efforts?**

➤ **What community and school variables will be barriers to the school improvement efforts? How will you address this?**

These reflection questions will empower school leaders to successfully implement any reform or school improvement efforts.

Empowering the Heart, Empowers You!

The goal of my writing has been to empower educators with illuminating insights and strategies that can help them to create a more empowered school. In closing, I want to share empowering words that I hope every educator takes to heart.

Empowering for School Leaders – Understand that every school is different. To empower a school means you must empower its community to sustain school improvement.

Empowering for School Personnel – Understand that every student is different. To empower a student means you must remove barriers and encourage the student's progress.

Empowering for Parents/Community – Understand that every community is different. To empower our children, we must create an environment where children are given multiple opportunities to develop their passion and learn to face adversity and overcome these obstacles.

Empowering for Students – Understand you are an individual. Your identity is your passion. Your passion resides in your heart and it is your gift. The heartbeat is your constant reminder of the gift you have in your heart. When you share your gift with the world. You are empowered!

The front cover of this book has the heart shaped by a stethoscope. The physician uses the stethoscope tool to understand the condition of the patient on the inside. An effective physician is able to diagnose problems, prescribe treatments and empower patients to improve themselves – all from a thorough assessment of the patient both inside and out. The effective physician would never mass produce a diagnosis and treatment because she understands the conditions of each of her patients is totally different from the rest. I encourage educators to use their "educational stethoscope" to search the individual passions and purpose of each child and empower them to turn their passion into a gift for others. This is the power of an educated heart.

As a high school principal, I had the honor of handing students their diplomas at the graduation ceremony each year. For my address to the students I would write an original poem about their school year and the accomplishments of their class. In the poem I included life lessons that I hoped they would carry forward. In the spirit of carrying my message forward, I am concluding this book with a poem.

As we travel along life's journey,
Challenges will come by day and night,
Yet Joy seems tied to conditions,
Absent in the Storm, present in the Light.

For the Storm knows its mission,
The Wind, Rain and Thunder have joined it's ranks,
The Storm comes to steal your Joy,
In its midst, Are YOU empowered to give thanks?

From where does this power come,
The answer is one of three parts,
We are Mind, Body and Spirit
The latter powers our Hearts.

The goal of education, let me overview
By the end of schooling I pray you knew,
The question, to the mirror, Who Are You?
Learning is not something just to get through
The process matters in the things you do,
So when you fail once, smile on take two,
For the purpose of life, inside is the best clue,
Our heart has the power, we appeal to.

This power can defeat the Storm,
It can remove the clouds of doubt,
This Power grows with Faith works,
Measured by quality inside not out.

Let your Light shine, but not for credit of men,
Light nurtures the seeds of faith, the Spirit within.
For Heaven doesn't recognize the size of the tree,
It rejoices from the fruit on each branch we see.

The greatest Teacher seeks your Heart,
And directs you toward your gift,
So be an inspiration for others,
Use your life to serve and uplift.

As we travel along life's journey,
We will stumble and we will fall,
Remember, Love conquers ALL Storms,
Because the Heart EMPOWERS Us All!

— Dr. Akil E. Ross

⩗⩗⩗ REFERENCES ⩗⩗⩗

Adler, A., Ansbacher, H. and Ansbacher, R. (2006). *The individual psychology of Alfred Adler.* New York: HarperPerennial.

Adler, A. and Radin, P. (2014). *Practice and theory of individual psychology.* London: Routledge.

Baum, L. F. (1904). *The wonderful Wizard of Oz / by L. Frank Baum; with pictures by W. W. Denslow.* G. M. Hill Co.

Clifton, J. (2011). *The Coming Jobs War.* New York, NY: Gallup Press.

College Completion. (2015). The Chronicle of Higher Education, Retrieved April 14, 2019, from https://collegecompletion.chronicle.com/

Collins, J. (2001). *Good to Great.* New York: Harper Business.

Csikszentmihalyi, M. (2009). *Flow.* New York: Harper [and] Row.

Dweck, C. (2008). *Mindset.* New York: Ballantine.

Flach, T. (2017, October 27) He flunked third grade. Now he's the best high school principal in the nation. https://www.thestate.com/news/local/education/article181130861.html

Freire, P. (2000). *Pedagogy of the oppressed.* New York: Continuum.

Friedman, T. and Mandelbaum, M. (2012). *That used to be us.* New York: Picador.

REFERENCES

Fuller, E., Pendola, A., Young, M. (2018, January) Policy Brief 2018-2: The role of principals in reducing teacher turnover and the shortage of teachers. University Counsel for Educational Administration. 1-2.

Gleason, D. (2017). *At What Cost? Defending adolescent development in fiercely competitive schools:* Developmental Empathy, LLC.

Goldin, C. (1999, August). A brief history of education in the United States. Cambridge. National Bureau of Economic Research.

King. M.L. J, (1968, February) The drum major instinct. Delivered at Ebenezer Baptist Church. Retrieved 4/19 https://kinginstitute.stanford.edu/king-papers/documents/drum-major-instinct-sermon-delivered-ebenezer-baptist-church

Kotter, J. P. (2012). *Leading change.* Boston: Harvard Business Review Press.

Ladson-Billings, G. (2009). *The Dreamkeepers.* San Francisco, Calif.: Jossey-Bass Publishers.

Layton, L. (2015, October 24). Study says standardized testing is overwhelming nation's public schools. *The Washington Post.* Education

Lencioni, P. (2002). *The five corruptions of a team.* San Francisco, Calif.: Jossey-Bass.

⟋⟍⟍⟋⟍⟋ REFERENCES ⟋⟍⟍⟋⟍⟋

McFarland, J., Cui, J., and Stark, P. (2018). Trends in High School Dropout and Completion Rates in the United States: 2014 (NCES 2018-117). U.S. Department of Education. Washington, DC: National Center for Education Statistics. Retrieved 4/19 from http://nces.ed.gov/pubsearch.

Moffitt, E. Et al. (2011). A Gradient of Childhood Self-Control Predicts Health, Wealth, and Public Safety. Proceedings of the National Academy of Sciences of the United States of America. 108. 2693-8. 10.1073/pnas.1010076108

Ozersky, J. (2017). *Colonel Sanders and the American Dream.* [S.l.]: Univ of Texas Press.

Reilly, K. (2018, September). The Life of the American Teacher: High demands. Low Pay. And a long fight ahead. *Time*, 192(12). pp. 26–33.

Rethink School (2018) Office of Career, Technical and Adult Education. United States Department of Education. Retrieved 4/19 https://sites.ed.gov/octae/files/2018/12/RethinkCTE.pdf

Rothstein, R. (2004). *Class and schools.* [New York, N.Y.]: Teachers College, Columbia University.

Schmoker, M. (2011). *Focus.* Alexandria, Va.: ASCD.

Schrobsdorff, S. (2016, November). Teen Depression and Anxiety: Why the kids are not alright. Time, 188(19).

Senge, P. (2006). *The fifth discipline*. London: Random House Business.

Sinek, S. (2013). *Start with why: How great leaders inspire everyone to take action*. London: Portfolio/Penguin.

Sorkin, A. R. (2018). *Too big to fail: The inside story of how Wall Street and Washington fought to save the financial system--and themselves*. New York: Penguin Books.

Washington, B. (2008). *The story of my life and work*. New York: Barnes & Noble.

Weiss, D. (2017, October 2). The forgetting curve and how to improve your memory. https://www.timetoknow.com/blog/how_to_improve_your_memory/

Woodson, C. G. (1990). *The Mis-education of the Negro*. Trenton, N.J: Africa World Press.

Photo Credit: Eli Warren

"He flunked the third grade. Now he's the best high school principal in the nation." This was the headline from the local newspaper after he was announced the National Principal of the Year. Dr. Akil Ross' story is a testimony of the power a community has to transform a struggling student into a high performing student. Akil grew up in Washington, DC during the height of a drug and crime wave that claimed the potential of many young people in his community. In the midst of these conditions, transformational elements were made available that empowered him to maximize his potential. He credits his home, his elementary school and a recreational center for teaching him how to face adversity and overcome obstacles early in his life. As a result of the high expectations set in his home, school and on the playing field, Akil was able to earn a full scholarship to Duke University.

Upon graduation from Duke University, Akil moved to South Carolina, where he taught social studies for three years at Eau Claire High School in Columbia, SC. In 2005, he obtained his M.Ed. in Secondary Educational Administration from the University of South Carolina and joined Chapin High School as an assistant principal in July of 2005. After

5 years as an assistant principal, he was named principal in July of 2010. In July of 2012, he earned a doctorate degree in Curriculum Studies from the University of South Carolina.

Chapin High School received many awards and recognitions under Akil's leadership, such as the Palmetto's Finest Award, Blue Ribbon Schools of Excellence Lighthouse Award, several national rankings in academics from *Newsweek, Niche, Washington Post* and *US News & World Report*. His school earned 20 State Championships in 8 Years (14 State Championships in Athletics, 4 State Championships in Marching Band and 2 NJROTC State Championships as well as 1 National Championship). As principal of Chapin High School, Dr. Ross was named the 2017 South Carolina Secondary Principal of the Year and the 2018 NASSP National Principal of the Year.

He and his wife Jocelyn live in Columbia, SC and have two children, Alyssa and A.J. Dr. Ross started HeartEd, LLC, an educational consulting company, to share lessons and strategies to further his vision of a future where every community Empowers every child.

Dr. Ross is available for speaking engagements and consulting. You can contact him via email at empower@heartedllc.org. Visit his webpage www.heartedllc.org and follow him on Twitter @DrRoss_Akil.